CliffsN

Kn

A Separate Peace

**By Charles Higgins, Ph.D.,
and Regina Higgins, Ph.D.**

IN THIS BOOK

- ■ Learn about the Life and Background of the Author

- ■ Preview an Introduction to the Novel

- ■ Explore themes, character development, and recurring images in the Critical Commentaries

- ■ Examine in-depth Character Analyses

- ■ Acquire an understanding of the novel with Critical Essays

- ■ Reinforce what you learn with CliffsNotes Review

- ■ Find additional information to further your study in the CliffsNotes Resource Center and online at www.cliffsnotes.com

IDG Books Worldwide, Inc.
An International Data Group Company
Foster City, CA • Chicago, IL • Indianapolis, IN • New York, NY

About the Author

Charles and Regina Higgins have worked together as educational writers for 15 years. They both have Ph.D.s in English from Indiana University.

Publisher's Acknowledgments

Editorial

Project Editor: Kelly Ewing
Acquisitions Editor: Greg Tubach
Editorial Coordinator: Michelle Hacker
Glossary Editors: The Editors and staff of Webster's New World Dictionaries

Production

Indexer: York Production Services
Proofreader: York Production Services
IDG Books Indianapolis Production Department

CliffsNotes™ Knowles' *A Separate Peace*
Published by
IDG Books Worldwide, Inc.
An International Data Group Company
919 E. Hillsdale Blvd.
Suite 400
Foster City, CA 94404

www.idgbooks.com (IDG Books Worldwide Web site)

www.cliffsnotes.com (CliffsNotes Web site)

ISBN: 0-7645-8578-9

Printed in the United States of America

10 9 8 7 6 5 4 3 2 1

1V/SU/QV/QQ/IN

Distributed in the United States by IDG Books Worldwide, Inc.

Distributed by CDG Books Canada Inc. for Canada; by Transworld Publishers Limited in the United Kingdom; by IDG Norge Books for Norway; by IDG Sweden Books for Sweden; by IDG Books Australia Publishing Corporation Pty. Ltd. for Australia and New Zealand; by TransQuest Publishers Pte Ltd. for Singapore, Malaysia, Thailand, Indonesia, and Hong Kong; by Gotop Information Inc. for Taiwan; by ICG Muse, Inc. for Japan; by Intersoft for South Africa; by Eyrolles for France; by International Thomson Publishing for Germany, Austria and Switzerland; by Distribuidora Cuspide for Argentina; by LR International for Brazil; by Galileo Libros for Chile; by Ediciones ZETA S.C.R. Ltda. for Peru; by WS Computer Publishing Corporation, Inc., for the Philippines; by Contemporanea de Ediciones for Venezuela; by Express Computer Distributors for the Caribbean and West Indies; by Micronesia Media Distributor, Inc. for Micronesia; by Chips Computadoras S.A. de C.V. for Mexico; by Editorial Norma de Panama S.A. for Panama; by American Bookshops for Finland.

For general information on IDG Books Worldwide's books in the U.S., please call our Consumer Customer Service department at **800-762-2974**. For reseller information, including discounts and premium sales, please call our Reseller Customer Service department at **800-434-3422**.

For information on where to purchase IDG Books Worldwide's books outside the U.S., please contact our International Sales department at **317-596-5530** or fax **317-572-4002**.

For consumer information on foreign language translations, please contact our Customer Service department at **1-800-434-3422**, fax 317-572-4002, or e-mail rights@idgbooks.com.

For information on licensing foreign or domestic rights, please phone **+1-650-653-7098**.

For sales inquiries and special prices for bulk quantities, please contact our Order Services department at **800-434-3422** or write to the address above.

For information on using IDG Books Worldwide's books in the classroom or for ordering examination copies, please contact our Educational Sales department at **800-434-2086** or fax 317-572-4005.

For press review copies, author interviews, or other publicity information, please contact our Public Relations department at **650-653-7000** or fax 650-653-7500.

For authorization to photocopy items for corporate, personal, or educational use, please contact Copyright Clearance Center, 222 Rosewood Drive, Danvers, MA 01923, or fax **978-750-4470**.

Library of Congress Cataloging-in-Publication Data

Higgins, Charles.
    CliffsNotes A Separate Peace / by Charles Higgins and Regina Higgins.
        p. cm.
    ISBN 0-7645-8578-9 (alk. paper)
    1. Knowles, John, 1926-. Separate Peace--Examinations--Study guides. 2. Preparatory school students in literature. I. Higgins, Regina Kirby. II. Title.

PS3561 .N68 S4345 2000
813'.54--dc21   00-039689
                                                      CIP

is a registered trademark under exclusive license to IDG Books Worldwide, Inc. from International Data Group, Inc.

Table of Contents

Life and Background of the Author 1

Personal Background 2

    Early Years 2

    Education 2

    Jobs 2

    Literary Writing 2

    Honors and Awards 3

Introduction to the Novel 4

Introduction 5

    A Brief Synopsis 6

List of Characters 8

Character Map 10

Critical Commentaries 11

    Chapter 1 12

    Chapter 2 15

    Chapter 3 19

    Chapter 4 23

    Chapter 5 27

    Chapter 6 30

    Chapter 7 34

    Chapter 8 39

    Chapter 9 44

    Chapter 10 48

    Chapter 11 52

    Chapter 12 56

    Chapter 13 60

Character Analysis 63

    Gene Forrester 64

    Phineas (Finny) 65

    Brinker Hadley 66

    Elwin (Leper) Lepellier 67

Critical Essays **68**
    From Innocence to Experience 69
    Gene and Finny: Doubles 71

CliffsNotes Review **75**
    Identify the Quote 75
    Essay Questions 76
    Practice Projects 77

CliffsNotes Resource Center **78**
    Books 78
    Internet 79
    Films and Other Recordings 79
    Journals 79
    Send Us Your Favorite Tips 80

Index **81**

How to Use This Book

CliffsNotes Knowles' *A Separate Peace* supplements the original work, giving you background information about the author, an introduction to the novel, a graphical character map, critical commentaries, expanded glossaries, and a comprehensive index. CliffsNotes Review tests your comprehension of the original text and reinforces learning with questions and answers, practice projects, and more. For further information on John Knowles and *A Separate Peace*, check out the CliffsNotes Resource Center.

CliffsNotes provides the following icons to highlight essential elements of particular interest:

Reveals the underlying themes in the work.

Helps you to more easily relate to or discover the depth of a character.

Uncovers elements such as setting, atmosphere, mystery, passion, violence, irony, symbolism, tragedy, foreshadowing, and satire.

Enables you to appreciate the nuances of words and phrases.

Don't Miss Our Web Site

Discover classic literature as well as modern-day treasures by visiting the CliffsNotes Web site at www.cliffsnotes.com. You'll find interactive tools that are fun and informative, links to interesting Web sites, and additional resources to help you continue your learning.

At www.cliffsnotes.com, you can obtain a quick download of a CliffsNotes title, purchase a title in print form, browse our catalog, or view samples such as a table of contents or a character map quickly and easily. See you at www.cliffs notes.com!

LIFE AND BACKGROUND OF THE AUTHOR

Personal Background 2

Personal Background

John Knowles won both critical and popular success with his first novel, *A Separate Peace*. In the 40 years since its publication, the novel has become a classic for both young adults and adult readers. Although he has written eight other novels, including *Peace Breaks Out*, which shares the prep school setting of the earlier novel, Knowles has not yet repeated the success of his first work. The author's reputation as a writer of fiction still rests on *A Separate Peace*.

Early Years

Knowles was born in 1926, in Fairmont, West Virginia. He spent his childhood in the small town of a coal-mining region, attending public schools. At 15, he left Fairmont for Phillips Exeter Academy, an elite prep school in New Hampshire. Knowles found Exeter both socially and academically challenging, and his experiences there inspired at least two of his later works: *A Separate Peace* (1959) and *Peace Breaks Out* (1981), in which Exeter is reconceived as Devon School.

Education

Knowles graduated early from Exeter in August 1947 because of his participation in the summer Anticipatory Program, a special wartime term, like Devon's Summer Session, meant to prepare boys for military service. In the fall of 1944, Knowles entered Yale University to study English. After serving for eight months in the U.S. Army Air Corps, Knowles returned to Yale, receiving a Bachelor of Arts degree in 1949.

Jobs

After graduating from college, Knowles worked as a reporter for the *Hartford Courant* and occasionally wrote theater reviews for the newspaper. By 1952, he was a freelance writer, with several articles published in *Holiday* magazine, where he became an associate editor. The success of *A Separate Peace* gave Knowles the financial freedom to devote himself entirely to writing fiction.

Literary Writing

Early in his career, Knowles wrote a novel that was never published and a short story that appeared in a small fiction magazine. He began to experiment with the material that would inspire the early chapters of *A Separate Peace* with the short story "Phineas," published in *Cosmopolitan* in 1956.

Knowles submitted his completed novel to American publishers, but the manuscript was rejected. Knowles found a British publisher, Secker and Warburg, for his work. *A Separate Peace* appeared in 1959 and quickly earned the praise of British reviewers. By the spring of 1960, when the New York edition came out, American critics were acclaiming the novel as well.

The success of the novel freed Knowles to write and to travel. His next two books, the novel *Morning in Antibes* (1962) and *Double Vision: American Thoughts from Abroad* (1964), a collection of travel essays, take for their inspiration Knowles' wanderings on the Riviera and in the Middle East.

With *Indian Summer* (1966), Knowles returned to the theme of boyhood friendships he had explored in *A Separate Peace*, but critics declared the new novel a disappointment compared to Knowles' first great work. Knowles found a new subject and tone in *Spreading Fires* (1974), a gothic thriller set on the Riviera. He explored the effects of the past on the present in *A Stolen Past* (1983) and *The Private Life of Axie Reed* (1986). His West Virginia childhood inspired *A Vein of Riches* (1978), a historical novel about coal mining.

Returning to New England themes, Knowles set *The Paragon* (1971) at Yale University and then finally came back to the fictional Devon School with *Peace Breaks Out* (1981). Again, critics praised the author's craft, but most agreed that the best novel written by Knowles was his first, *A Separate Peace*.

Honors and Awards

A Separate Peace won Knowles the Richard and Hinda Rosenthal Foundation Award from the National Institute of Arts and Letters. The work also received the William Faulkner Award for the most promising first novel of 1960. In 1961, Knowles accepted the National Association of Independent Schools Award.

INTRODUCTION TO THE NOVEL

Introduction 5

List of Characters 8

Character Map 10

Introduction

John Knowles' best-known work, *A Separate Peace*, remains one of the most popular post-war novels about adolescence. Although set in World War II, the novel explores a crucial cultural theme of the '50s, the motivations of a young man making a troubled transition from childhood to adulthood. Like the novels *Lord of the Flies* and *Catcher in the Rye*, as well as the film *Rebel Without a Cause*, *A Separate Peace* dramatizes the challenge of growing up to be a truly individual adult in a conformist world.

World War II provides the novel's historical backdrop, a time when young men anticipated the enforced conformity and danger of war service. Fifteen million American men joined the military during World War II, with universal service accepting virtually all young men 18 and older who stood taller than five feet and weighed more than 105 pounds.

About two-thirds (about ten million) of the men serving were drafted, and most of them were sent to the infantry, where they saw the worst of the war, and endured the highest casualty rate. The smaller group—still, about five million—enlisted, and so could choose the branch of service they would join. In Knowles' novel, the boys of the Devon School, educated, with families that are comfortable, if not wealthy, choose enlistment in relatively prestigious (and safer) training programs in preference to the draft.

But, drafted or enlisted, the recruit had to look forward to the same period of basic training, when individual differences were supposed to be discarded to make way for the new group identity and goals. In Knowles' novel, this transition from a small prep school to military service looms as a big adjustment, one that proves too much for one Devon student.

After the war was won, forms of military life seemed to continue in American culture. The commander of the troops in Europe, General Eisenhower, became president. American industries designed their corporate structures along military lines. Dress codes flourished, and army regulation haircuts for men were popular even with younger people. Social conformity was the rule, and individuality raised suspicion.

In the fiction of the '50s, adolescents emerged as the ultimate individuals—people who constantly tested the rules or sought to live without them. Holden Caulfield, the protagonist of *Catcher in the Rye*, aimlessly wanders New York after being expelled (again) from prep school. The British boys of *Lord of the Flies*, shipwrecked on an island, create their own unique combination of anarchy and tyranny when the structure of their conventional world collapses.

In contrast, the characters of *A Separate Peace* remain within the defining and confining world of their prep school, where wealth and privilege enforce high expectations for conventional behavior. The main characters, Gene and Finny, carve out their own world within the school, taking advantage of a relatively casual summer semester, when the masters loosen their grip on the boys. The world of Devon's Summer Session becomes their personal paradise, which, like the biblical Eden, comes to an end with a tree and a fall.

Finny's fall from the tree and Gene's fall from innocence can be traced to unresolved tensions in Gene over conformity and individuality, created by the mixed feeling of envy and admiration he feels for Finny. A true individual, Finny enjoys pure freedom, an inspired, natural flow of energy that expresses itself in his athletic strength and grace. Gene, in contrast, feels the constraints of conformity, obedience, and responsibility. As a hard-working, serious student, Gene resents Finny's effortless life and especially his good nature.

Motivated, then, by envy and resentment, Gene causes Finny to fall from a high limb and break his leg, ending his friend's sports career and, ultimately, his life. After the fall, Gene's unacknowledged guilt haunts him, then moves him to painful self-knowledge, and at last to a peace that lights his way into adulthood.

A Brief Synopsis

In the late 1950s, 15 years after graduation, Gene Forrester returns to Devon, an elite prep school in New Hampshire. Walking through the campus in the cold November mist, Gene remembers his experiences at Devon during World War II, especially the Summer Session of 1942, when he was 16 years old.

At a tree by the river, Gene thinks of his friend and roommate, Phineas (nicknamed Finny), the best athlete in the school. As the story moves into the past, Finny jumps from a high limb of the tree into the river—an activity forbidden to all but the oldest Devon boys—and dares Gene to jump as well. Gene jumps, but is frightened. Finny, however, takes such delight in the dangerous, forbidden jump that he forms the

Suicide Society and invites all the Devon boys to test their courage by jumping from the tree into the river. At each initiation, Gene and Finny make the first jump, but Gene never gets over his fear.

Finny's status as the best athlete inspires Gene to strive to become the best student in the school. Gene applies himself to his studies seriously, but feels pressure from Finny to join in his activities, especially the Suicide Society. After failing a math test because of a forbidden trip to the beach, Gene suspects that Finny is deliberately trying to sabotage his studying. This silent resentment builds until the end of the summer, when Finny insists that Gene leave his books to jump from the tree again. High in the tree with his friend, Gene impulsively jounces the limb and causes Finny to fall.

Finny's shattered leg ends his involvement in sports, a consequence that brings the guilty and fearful Gene to tears. Once in the infirmary and again at Finny's home, where he is recovering, Gene tries to confess that he caused the fall. But Finny's trust in Gene is absolute, and he refuses to believe the confession.

Without Finny around, Gene grows closer to Brinker Hadley, a student leader who teases him with the accusation that he got rid of Finny to have their room to himself. Brinker's joking frightens and angers Gene, but his new friend's energy also inspires him. One night, after Brinker announces his intention to enlist immediately, Gene decides to enter military service as well, a resolution that disappears suddenly upon Finny's return.

Finny tells Gene that he must become an athlete for both of them and proposes to train him for the 1944 Olympics. When Gene tries to explain that the war will most certainly make the Olympics impossible, Finny announces that the war is a fake. Finny's dream of the 1944 Olympics becomes a shared reality between the friends as the former athlete trains his replacement. Gene joins his friend in a peaceful retreat from the world, celebrated in the school's (unofficial) Winter Carnival.

Even a friend's enlistment and emotional breakdown does not intrude upon the peace Gene finds with Finny, until one evening when Brinker and some of the other boys drag Gene and Finny to the Assembly Room, where they propose to get to the truth about Finny's injury. In a mock trial, Brinker questions Finny, searching for proof of Gene's responsibility in his fall. When another boy's memory of the fall opens Finny's eyes to his friend's guilt, he lurches angrily from the room, falling on the stairs and breaking his leg again.

At a distance, Gene follows Finny to the infirmary, hoping to talk with him alone. Finny, however, will not talk with Gene until the next day, when he asks sadly if his friend really meant to hurt him or if it were simply an unconscious impulse. Gene insists that he acted without hatred—blindly—and Finny accepts the explanation with relief. Later that day, in an operation to set the leg again, Finny dies when some marrow from the broken bone enters the bloodstream and stops his heart. Gene accepts the news without crying, because he feels as if he has died, too.

Later, after the war, Gene looks back and understands that he fought his real war at Devon. Gene's true enemy was the narrow, spiteful self that harbored jealousy, and that self died with Finny.

List of Characters

Gene Forrester The narrator, Finny's roommate and best friend. Gene unfolds the painful story of his growth in a New England prep school during World War II, when his jealousy caused Finny's tragic fall.

Phineas (Finny) Gene's roommate and best friend. A gifted athlete, Finny represents freedom and good nature. His fall from the tree ends his competition in sports and ultimately costs him his life.

Elwin Lepellier (Leper) A shy student with an interest in nature and skiing, a friend of Gene's. The first Devon student from his class to enlist, Leper suffers a mental breakdown in the army. Leper's memory of the fall reveals Gene's guilt to Finny.

Brinker Hadley A student leader, friend of Gene. When Finny leaves school to recover from his fall, Brinker temporarily takes his place as Gene's closest friend. Controlling and aggressive, Brinker organizes the "investigation" into Finny's accident that becomes, in effect, Gene's trial.

Mr. Hadley Brinker's father, who appears near the conclusion of the novel. Mr. Hadley's hearty enthusiasm for the war makes clear the distance of the older generation from the boys, who view the war and their part in it with reluctance and dread.

Mr. Prud'homme A Devon master, or teacher. Charmed by Finny and lulled by the casual atmosphere of the Summer Session, he does not enforce the usual school discipline.

Mr. Ludsbury A strict Devon master, a contrast to Mr. Prud'homme. During the Winter Session, he strives to bring the boys back to the traditional rules. He represents discipline and devotion to duty.

Dr. Stanpole The school physician. He cares for Finny in the infirmary after his accident and performs surgery to set Finny's leg, an operation that Finny does not survive. Responsible and capable, Dr. Stanpole nevertheless cannot help the young man. His failure reflects the powerlessness of older adults at a time of war.

Phil Latham The wrestling coach who assists Dr. Stanpole when Finny falls the second time. He offers to talk with Gene about Finny's accident, but Gene changes the subject. Like Dr. Stanpole, Latham represents the sympathetic, but powerless, adult.

Character Map

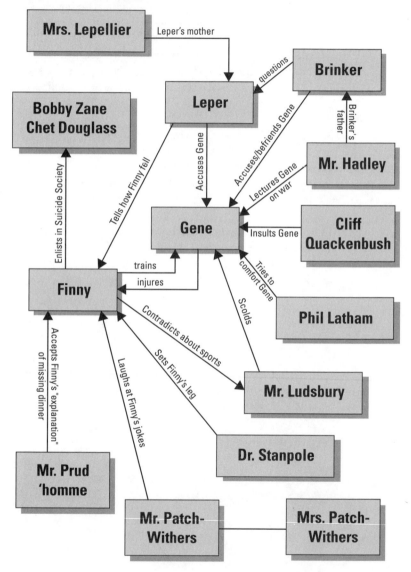

CRITICAL
COMMENTARIES

Chapter 1 12

Chapter 2 15

Chapter 3 19

Chapter 4 23

Chapter 5 27

Chapter 6 30

Chapter 7 34

Chapter 8 39

Chapter 9 44

Chapter 10 48

Chapter 11 52

Chapter 12 56

Chapter 13 60

Chapter 1

Summary

As the novel opens, Gene Forrester returns to Devon, the New Hampshire boarding school he attended during World War II. Gene has not seen Devon for 15 years, and so he notices the ways in which the school has changed since he was a student there. Strangely, the school seems newer, but perhaps, he thinks, the buildings are just better taken care of now that the war is over.

Gene walks through the campus on a bleak, rainy November afternoon, revisiting the buildings and fields he remembers—and especially two places he recalls as "fearful sites." At the First Academic Building, he enters the foyer to look closely at the white marble steps. Then he trudges across the playing fields to the river in search of a particular tree and finally recognizes it by its long limb over the water and the scars on its trunk. The tree, he thinks, is smaller than he remembers. The chapter section ends with Gene heading back to shelter through the rain.

The second section opens during the summer of 1942 when Gene is 16. He is attending a special Summer Session at Devon, designed to speed up education to prepare the boys for the military draft in their senior year.

Gene stands at the same tree with his best friend and roommate, Phineas (nicknamed Finny), and three other boys, Elwin Lepellier (Leper), Chet Douglass, and Bobby Zane. The tree seems enormous to Gene, but Finny suddenly decides to climb it and jump into the river, just like the Devon 17 year olds, who are training for military service. Finny jumps and dares Gene to follow. Against his better judgment, Gene climbs the tree and also jumps, but the three others refuse.

The shared danger of jumping brings Finny and Gene closer. While the rest of the boys hurry ahead at the sound of the bell for dinner, the roommates playfully wrestle until they are late for the meal. They slip into the dormitory, where they read their English assignments and play their radio (against school rules), until it is time for bed.

Commentary

Theme

A Separate Peace tells a story of initiation—the account of Gene Forrester's growth from adolescence into adulthood during World War II.

The novel opens with the narrator, Gene, returning to his old prep school Devon. Significantly, he makes his visit alone, not as part of an official homecoming or alumni reunion. The visit is private, his goal personal—to revisit two "fearful sites" from his youth. In encountering the past, Gene hopes to understand the crucial events that shaped his adulthood, in order to face them and finally move beyond them.

Gene's recognition of the changes in Devon shows the ways he himself has changed. The beauty of the campus still impresses him, even in a cold rain, but the school itself seems like "a museum," a place to observe rather than to inhabit. Gene has grown beyond his school and is no longer a part of it; yet the school and his memories of what happened here continue to shape him in ways he feels compelled to explore and finally to understand.

Literary Device

The two "fearful sites" Gene visits—a marble staircase inside the First Academic Building and a tree by the river—sharply contrast with each other. The tree, gnarled and old, represents an integral part of nature, simplicity itself, while the marble staircase, beautifully formed and decorated, expresses a highly polished culture. The two sites seem to show the double nature of Devon—natural landscape and rich interiors.

Style & Language

The narration makes clear that the tree and the stairs hold great, even terrifying significance for Gene, but the chapter gives no indication of what might have happened here. Gene's past, the narrator hints, somehow unites these two very different places. The intriguing combination sparks curiosity about the story that will unfold in the novel.

Gene contemplates the "hardness" of the marble stairway in the First Academic Building and then takes an intent walk toward the tree through the rain and fog—a trek that ruins a pair of expensive shoes in the mud. This sacrifice emphasizes the importance of his visit, just as his determined push to the river represents a journey into the past, the mud symbolizing the messy, unresolved events from long ago that stick to him, and even threaten to pull him down.

But when Gene arrives at the second "fearful site"—the tree—he finds that it has lost at least some of its power for him. The tree, like

Devon, has changed because Gene has changed. The tree seems smaller than he remembers, much less isolated and imposing, because he has grown in height, and the tree has also been shriveled by age. Relieved, changed, Gene leaves the tree, his revisiting accomplished, his fears put finally to rest.

But while the adult Gene makes peace with himself in the present, the tree itself pivots the story back into the past. Like a cinematic effect, the image of the adult Gene dissolves as the young Gene emerges, an indication that the novel will not be an adult's retelling of past events, but a reliving of the experience through the young boy's eyes.

The fateful tree looms large in the past. Forbidden to all but the senior Devon boys training for war, it stands as a challenge and even, imaginatively, as a matter of life and death. It recalls, symbolically, the forbidden tree in the Garden of Eden and the Fall of Man. Great and tragic changes traditionally take place under (or in) such trees.

Under this tree, Gene and Finny now appear together, their physical similarities underscored, even down to height and weight; and yet, as the scene progresses, their fundamental differences emerge. Finny shows himself to be adventurous, witty, unconcerned with the rules, while Gene proves to be more thoughtful and less daring than his friend. This first look at both boys, including their jumps from the tree limb, dramatizes the fact that Finny will be the heroic character of the novel.

Gene's uncertainty, his unwilling obedience, and his sudden euphoria after the jump represent an early expression of the mixed feelings he has for Finny. Finny has power over Gene, and Gene quietly resents this power. Unwilling to challenge his friend directly, Gene works out his repressed anger in the horseplay at the end of the chapter, knocking Finny to the ground. Finny responds playfully, but the physical struggle between the boys foreshadows another struggle that will end in tragedy.

Glossary

(Here and in the following sections, difficult words and phrases are explained.)

Leper a person having leprosy; a person to be shunned or ostracized, as because of the danger of moral contamination. Here, it is a nickname for the quiet, aloof Elwin Lepellier.

seigneurs lord here, the term characterizes the superiority Gene and Finny feel when they jump from the tree and the others do not.

Chapter 2

Summary

The morning after the boys first jump from the tree, Mr. Prud'homme, a substitute Master for the summer, scolds Gene and Finny for missing dinner. Finny tells Mr. Prud'homme that they were late because they were jumping out of the tree to prepare for military service—a far-fetched excuse he weaves into a long, funny explanation. Finny's friendly chatter charms Mr. Prud'homme, and the Master lets the boys off without punishment.

That day Finny wears a very un-Devon bright pink shirt, and its unconventional color draws Gene's attention. The shirt, Finny insists, is an "emblem"—a celebration of the first Allied bombing of Central Europe. Later, at a formal tea, Finny wins over the strict Mr. Patch-Withers with his "emblem." Finny even gets an appreciative laugh from the faculty and their wives when they see that he has also used his Devon tie as a belt, a gesture of disrespect for which anyone else would have been punished.

After the tea, Gene and Finny walk across the playing fields talking. Finny declares that he does not believe the Allies bombed Central Europe, and Gene, surrounded by the peace and serenity of the elms, agrees. Bombs in Central Europe, Gene reflects, seem unreal to a boy at Devon.

As they approach the river, Finny dares Gene to jump out of the tree again. When Gene accepts, Finny offers to jump at the same time, to "cement" their "partnership." They also decide to form the Super Suicide Society of the Summer Session, in which all members will have to jump from the tree.

On the limb, Gene turns to talk to Finny and suddenly loses his balance. Instantly, Finny grabs Gene's arm, steadying him, and then both jump successfully into the river. Only later, after dinner, does Gene realize that Finny's quick response may have saved his life.

Commentary

Theme

As this chapter illustrates, Finny enjoys getting himself into tight (and sometimes dangerous) situations, and he relies on his natural charm and often illogical view of the world to extricate himself. While military service overtakes the older students, only the 16-year-old boys remain careless and happy in this peaceful world. For the masters of Devon—and Gene, too—Finny comes to represent the "essence of this careless peace."

Character Insight

While Finny likes to defy authority, play games, and jump out of trees—all of these essentially childish activities—Gene, by contrast, wants to become an adult and feels that he should learn how to live in the grown-up world. His basic nature points him in the direction of conventionality and conformity, and his instincts make him fear Finny's youthful spontaneity as dangerous—and yet also dangerously attractive.

As the chapter unfolds, Gene feels more and more caught in the irresistible pull of Finny's spontaneous nature, as well as his charismatic power to inspire people by creating his own imaginative world out of nothing more than his own whims. But Finny's ease at convincing others of his ideas also secretly galls Gene, who finds himself "unexpectedly" wishing to see his friend punished for his easy, winning ways of escaping trouble.

Literary Device

Finny's pink shirt stands as the central symbol of the chapter, the expression of his unique gift for making things mean what he wants them to mean. He chooses the pink shirt carelessly, as he does all his clothes, but once he puts it on, his inventive mind conjures up a reality for it that defies challenge, even when Gene offers his own typically conventional interpretation that people will think Finny is a "fairy." Finny calmly rejects Gene's objection and proposes instead his own eccentric idea, bridging the gap between reality and his whim with effortless grace. The pink shirt, he declares, is an "emblem" to celebrate the beginning of the Allied bombing of Central Europe.

Character Insight

At Mr. Patch-Withers' tea party, Finny's pink shirt—with the emblematic nature he ascribes to it—becomes his passport into the formal adult club that excludes and terrifies other students. While the other boys worry about making fools of themselves at this rather stiff and formal occasion, Finny proves himself calm and glib, his zany explanations coming from a sheer delight in talking freely, as a friend, with anyone, including the masters and their wives. In fact, his winning conversation, marked by casual grace and natural wit, charms everyone into accepting not only an unconventional piece of clothing, but his freely offered views on the war. Audaciously, Finny even talks his way out of a potentially disastrous situation when he casually reveals—to the horror of the headmaster's wife—that he is wearing his school tie as a belt.

But Finny's gift for talking himself out of trouble also arouses a strange spitefulness in Gene, who unconsciously desires to see his friend fail, and even, significantly, to fall. For example, Gene secretly delights at the prospect of Finny getting into trouble for wearing his school tie disrespectfully, but Gene's spirits deflate when the master laughingly accepts Finny's comical excuse. Even though it does not harm or even affect Gene, Finny's imaginative freedom seems to him an affront—an excess that must be punished.

Despite his resentment, though, Gene succumbs to Finny's charismatic power and persuasiveness. When Finny, in an imaginative reversal, declares his belief that there is no bombing in Europe, Gene comes to share in Finny's vision of a world set apart from conflict. As the two boys cross the forested campus on their way to the river, Gene gazes up at the sheltering elm trees, which seem to him to extend endlessly into the heavens and northward almost indefinitely. For Gene, at this moment, Devon—the "tame fringe of the last and greatest wilderness"— becomes a kind of Eden, where the thought of war seems impossible, even absurd.

But in the midst of this Eden, there already lurks deep in Gene's heart a type of original sin—his growing envy and resentment of Finny. Finny, though, remains unaware of his friend's true feelings and proposes that they climb the tree again and make the jump together. He means this double jump as a ritual act of friendship—a way of sealing the bond of their "partnership."

What happens next, on the limb before the boys jump, foreshadows the central dramatic event of the novel (in Chapter 4). Suddenly, Gene loses his balance—physically, of course, but symbolically, too— and Finny instinctively grasps his friend's hand to balance him and save him from falling.

Finny's action clearly reveals his true feelings for Gene; without even thinking, he reaches out to save his friend. Only later, after dinner, does Gene fully realize the danger from which Finny has saved him. The rush of gratitude and affection Gene feels seems to wash away the resentment about Finny's controlling influence.

As the novel progresses, though, Gene will move continually between these two emotions, further complicating his relationship with Finny—because, ironically, Gene has, in a sense, already fallen from Eden.

Chapter 3

Summary

As this chapter opens, Finny is recruiting the other boys for the Suicide Society. Every night, Gene and Finny jump from the tree and then watch their friends jump in order to join the club. This nightly meeting is the only scheduled activity Finny never misses. Gene goes along every time, but secretly he hates it.

Early in the summer, Finny becomes dissatisfied with the school sports program—badminton, in particular—and decides the boys should make up their own game (blitzball). He hurls a heavy medicine ball at Gene and challenges him to do something with it. Gene runs wildly with it, is tackled by the other boys, while Finny calls out plays, improvises rules on the run, and generally makes up the game as the boys play it. Chaotic blitzball turns out to be the hit of the summer, and Finny, naturally, proves to be the best player.

In the next section of the chapter, Gene remembers the time Finny broke the school swimming record. The two boys are alone in the pool when Finny notices a record from 1940 and decides to try to break it. With Gene as his timekeeper, Finny beats the record by .7 seconds, but there are no witnesses so the time will not count. When Gene encourages his friend to try again the next day to make it official, Finny refuses and asks Gene not to speak about it to anyone.

Finny then proposes a trip to the beach. Gene feels he should be studying for a trigonometry test, but agrees anyway. In violation of school rules, the boys ride their bicycles to the shore, where they swim in the ocean, eat hot dogs, drink beer, and sleep that night among the sand dunes. Just before falling asleep, Finny confides to Gene that he considers him his "best pal." Gene realizes that he should tell Finny he feels the same about him, but says nothing.

Commentary

In this chapter, Gene observes that Finny lives his life according to "inspiration and anarchy." But Gene, cautious and conventional, cannot finally abide such freedom.

Always the true innocent, Finny sees no difference, really, between his philosophy of life and his philosophy of sports. Sports, he paradoxically believes, produces only winners and never losers—and so it is with life, he assumes. Such radical innocence, as charming as it may be, threatens Gene and finally turns him away from Finny.

As the chapter opens, Gene begins to reconsider his double jump with Finny at the end of the previous chapter. Yes, Gene thinks, Finny saved his life, but it was because of Finny's insistent risk-taking that they found themselves in such a dangerous situation in the first place. Finny did not so much save his life, Gene concludes, as nearly get him killed.

Finny's inspired idea to form the Super Suicide Society simply compounds Gene's growing fears about their friendship, because the "suicide" here seems to suggest Gene's own possible self-destruction. According to the rules of the club, Finny and Gene must now jump from the tree every night, and Gene "hates" it. For Gene, the Suicide Club represents a kind of slow psychological suicide—the gradual loss of himself, as he sees his own identity eclipsed more and more with each evening's jump by Finny and his idea of life-threatening fun.

Like the Suicide Club, blitzball emerges as another physical manifestation of the anarchy inherent in Finny's nature. With blitzball, Finny playfully defies Devon authority (and its apparent affection for badminton), but at the same time the game also provides another source for Gene's growing jealousy and resentment of his friend. As Finny spontaneously invents the rules of the game on the run, blitzball seems to revolve mostly around Gene getting hit with a heavy medicine ball and repeatedly pummeled by the other players (appropriately called "enemies"). In contrast, Finny excels at blitzball, because he plays the game the same way he plays at life—by "reverses and deceptions and acts of sheer mass hypnotism."

Ironically, Finny invents the game of blitzball as a means of keeping the war at a distance during Devon's peaceful Summer Session, but the game—in an example of Finnian logic—paradoxically seems to have the reverse effect. The game's very name derives from the German *blitzkrieg* ("lightning war"), Nazi Germany's brutally swift attacks with aircraft and tanks in the early years of World War II. And one of blitzball's famous maneuvers—"Lepellier's Refusal"—foreshadows Leper's nervous breakdown and desertion from basic training later in the novel.

The war, in fact, casts its "olive drab" shadow across the world of Devon, but it is Gene's inner conflict—his jealousy and resentment of Finny—that finally darkens this chapter. Even in those moments when the two boys are closest, Gene finds himself threatened by Finny—by his athletic ability and natural grace, by his rebelliousness, and by his essential innocence.

Character Insight

For example, Gene cannot understand Finny's insistence on secrecy when the natural athlete suddenly breaks the school's swim record. Like his jumps from the tree and blitzball, Finny's feat at the pool embodies his idea of true sport—physical achievement for its own sake, uncompromised by adult authority. Finny breaks records—and rules—as a way of creating a world apart from the adults who serve the war. Indeed, in his various acts of defiance and athletic prowess, he conjures up an imaginative world where his own rules of freedom (and even anarchy) become the only rules.

Finny's disregard for official records or even keeping score baffles Gene and makes him worry about their friendship, since most relationships at Devon are based on rivalry. In contrast to Finny, Gene seeks the approval of authority and desires its formal acknowledgements—he wants to become valedictorian, after all.

Conventional in his thinking, Gene sees school and sports as formal competition—a public form of rivalry with clearly defined rules and expectations. As a result, he begins to wonder how he can be friendly rivals with someone who will not play by the rules, who stands so clearly superior to him, and who remains unassuming as well.

Tellingly, Gene flinches when Finny declares his friendship. This occurs on a forbidden trip to the ocean that Finny proposes in yet another example of his rebelliousness. Gene reluctantly goes along, although he resents the disruption in his ordered life and worries that it will mean that he will fail his trigonometry test (which he does).

Style & Language

When they arrive, Finny (as his name suggests) frolics effortlessly in the ocean, at one with its untamed force. But Gene finds himself thrown roughly about by the waves and retreats to the beach, where he worries that he will be expelled for this breach of the rules. Clearly, Finny's fun—a physical and mental state of being—remains beyond Gene's instincts and abilities.

The concluding scene at the ocean recalls the end of Chapter 2, when Finny grabs Gene's hand on the limb to steady him and also looks forward, darkly, to Gene's part in the fall that occurs at the close of Chapter 4. On the beach before sleep, in a moment of spontaneous candor, Finny offers Gene proof of his friendship when he calls him his "best pal." Although Gene realizes that he should reciprocate with his own profession of friendship, he doesn't reply, stopped "by that level of feeling, deeper than thought, which contains the truth."

Character Insight

At this moment, Gene realizes that his feelings for Finny are so bound up in jealousy and resentment that he cannot truly be friends with him. The results, dramatized in the next chapter, prove to be tragic.

Glossary

blitzkrieg sudden, swift, large-scale offensive warfare intended to win a quick victory, used by the Nazis. Here, the boys adapt the term for "blitzball," a game that emphasizes high energy and surprise manuevers.

Winston Churchill (1871–1947) British statesman and writer; prime minister (1940–45; 1951–55). Here, the boys refer to Churchill in his role as prime minister of Great Britain during World War II.

Josef Stalin (1879–1953) Soviet premier (1941–53); general secretary of the Communist party of the U.S.S.R. (1922–53). Here, the boys refer to Stalin in his role as leader of the Soviet Union during World War II.

Chapter 4

Summary

The boys ride back from the beach to Devon, arriving just in time for Gene's trigonometry test—the first examination Gene fails. Blitzball and the Suicide Society occupy the rest of the day and evening, and Gene begins to suspect that Finny is deliberately keeping him from studying. Instead of a "best pal," Gene begins to see his roommate as a deadly rival.

Finny already stands unchallenged as the best athlete at Devon, and Gene hopes to even up their status by becoming the best student. He sees Finny's games and rule-breaking—and even Finny's occasional studying—as a rival's sneaky attempts to make him fail.

The night before an important French examination, Finny announces that Leper is finally going to jump from the tree and so become a member of the Suicide Society. Unconvinced that Leper will jump and suspicious that Finny is really using this as an excuse to keep him from studying, Gene bursts out angrily at his roommate. Surprised and concerned, Finny tells Gene to stay and study, if that is what he wants to do.

But Gene goes to the tree, confused by thoughts that perhaps Finny is not his jealous rival after all. When they arrive at the tree, Finny proposes a double jump. Both boys climb the tree and stand on the limb above the river. Close to the trunk, Gene jounces the limb and watches Finny lose his balance and fall heavily to the bank. Then Gene walks out onto the limb and jumps easily into the river.

Commentary

Literary Device

Chapter 4 opens with the gray dawn and closes with a gray dusk, suggesting the symbolic unity of a single day (although a much greater time actually elapses). It begins, too, with Finny coming to life as Lazarus and ends with the tragic fall that destroys his life.

The chapter opens with the promise of the dawn over the ocean, with images of death gradually yielding to life as the sun rises to bring color to a gray world. As the Biblical allusions make clear, the sleeping Finny seems like Lazarus returned to life, and the white sand that surrounds the awakening boys recalls Eden.

Finny responds to this idyllic morning with characteristic action, proposing a quick swim. But in the dawn, by the roaring ocean, Gene can only think about limits and rules. A look at the rising sun tells him it is 6:30, and he worries that he will be late for his trigonometry test at 10:00.

For Gene, the meaning of the morning emerges not from the beauty of the dawn and the excitement of the waves, but from his worries and disappointments. He and Finny have lost their money, and they must now bicycle back to Devon without breakfast. In fact, they arrive at the school just in time for Gene to fail his examination.

By now, Gene suspects that Finny's innocent rule-breaking and time-wasting may serve a darker purpose. Inwardly, Gene hopes to become the best student in the school in order to make himself equal with Finny, who shines as the best athlete. This ambition invigorates Gene and allows him to think of his friendship with Finny as just another Devon rivalry. But when Finny teases him about studying and tries to get him to desert his books for fun, it seems to Gene that Finny secretly wants to see him fail.

Gene now decides that Finny must be his deadly rival, and that his playful roommate plans a deliberate plot to undermine the studying that Gene requires to become the best student in the school. But to keep this dark insight secret, Gene continues to go along on Finny's outings, including the nightly meetings of the Suicide Society, until one evening when Finny asks him to come to see Leper finally jump from the tree. Sullenly, Gene agrees to go, but he tells Finny angrily that it will ruin his chances for a good grade in French. Astonished that his friend must work to succeed at school, Finny tells Gene that he should stay and study, if he needs the time.

Finny's reaction, in its innocence and simplicity, overwhelms Gene, because he recognizes that Finny regards excellence in academics as a natural ability, just like his own agility and strength in sports. Finny does not mean to be his rival, Gene realizes, but is, instead, beyond the pettiness of rivalry.

And so, in Gene's view, Finny proves himself to be the better person. Paradoxically, by not playing the game of rivalry, Finny wins—or so it seems to Gene. This bitter knowledge goads Gene, and provokes him finally to violence against his friend.

The conclusion of the chapter, in which Finny falls from the tree, forms the dramatic center of the novel, because it expresses the truth of the boys' relationship—especially Gene's deepest feelings about Finny. While Finny helps Gene instinctively, in a moment too quick for thought, Gene, standing literally in the same place, hurts Finny grievously, in a response to a comparable, unconscious instinct. As Gene and Finny stand together on the limb, the scene recalls their earlier double jump, when Finny's quick action saves Gene from falling. But this time the boys' positions are reversed—Finny stands far out on the branch, while Gene stays safely near the trunk—and now Gene's knees bend (or so he remembers it), and he jounces the limb. Startled, off-balance, Finny falls heavily to the bank.

Fatefully, Gene's conflicted feelings find expression in a moment's gesture that destroys Finny's life. Temporarily relieved of his anger and jealousy, Gene jumps from the tree with confidence for the first time. The destruction of his deadly rival, it seems, liberates Gene to behave as Finny does—freely, easily, with unconscious grace.

This re-playing—yet reversal—of the earlier scene (from Chapter 2) makes clear the essential difference between the two boys. The tree reveals each boy's inner nature, and thus shows Gene the real difference between Finny and himself. This bitter knowledge, even more than the memory of Finny's injury, later makes the tree a "fearful site" for Gene.

Glossary

aide-memoire (French) a memorandum of a discussion, proposed agreement, etc. Here, Knowles uses the term comically.

Mahatma Gandhi (1869–1948) Mohandas Karamchand Gandhi, Hindu nationalist leader and social reformer, assassinated; called *Mahatma*. The term describes any of a class of wise and holy persons held in special regard or reverence. Here, Gene jokes that if Leper can find the courage to jump from the tree, than Gene is as holy as the Indian leader.

Ne Plus Ultra (Latin) the ultimate; especially the finest, best, most perfect, etc. Here the term refers to an academic award Gene hopes to win at graduation.

Lazarus the brother of Mary and Martha, raised from the dead by Jesus. Here, Finny awakening on the beach reminds Gene of Lazarus miraculously coming to life again.

Chapter 5

Summary

As the chapter opens, Gene hears from the school doctor, Dr. Stanpole, that Finny's leg has been "shattered" in the fall. Numbed by the terrible accident and fearing that he will be accused of causing it, Gene stays in his room. There he dresses in his roommate's clothes (including the pink shirt) and feels, for a time, as if he has become Finny — sharp, optimistic, confident. But when the moment passes, Gene again feels dread and guilt about what he has done to his friend.

After chapel one morning, Dr. Stanpole tells Gene that he may visit Finny in the infirmary. Finny is recovering, Dr. Stanpole explains to Gene, but he will never play in any sport again. Gene bursts into tears at the news. Gently, Dr. Stanpole encourages Gene to cheer up, for Finny's sake. Gene is the only person Finny has asked to see.

Gene arrives at the infirmary, certain that Finny will accuse him of causing the accident. In their conversation, Gene probes to see whether Finny realizes what made him fall. Although he has a vague sense of Gene's involvement in the accident, Finny pushes these thoughts aside and apologizes to his friend for suspecting him. Gene suddenly feels he must tell Finny the truth, but he is prevented by the arrival of Dr. Stanpole, who ends the visit.

That fall, on his way to Devon, Gene visits Finny in his home outside Boston, where he is still recuperating. There Gene admits jouncing the limb deliberately in order to make Finny fall. Finny refuses to believe his friend, and when Gene insists he is telling the truth, Finny tells him to go away.

Realizing that he is hurting Finny, Gene stops the talk, mumbling an excuse about being tired from the train ride. Finny tells Gene that he will return to Devon soon. The roommates part as friends, with Gene promising, falsely, that he will not start "living by the rules."

Commentary

This chapter presents the consequences of the fall, physically for Finny and psychologically for Gene. Here, as he tries to determine how much Finny actually knows about the fall, Gene begins a slow and torturous process to understand himself.

Although he is absorbed in his own grief in this chapter and fearful of discovery, Gene still senses the deep sadness the masters feel over Finny's injury. Such a tragedy seems to them especially cruel for a 16-year-old boy, who should be enjoying his last months of freedom before going to war. In fact, Finny's shattered leg becomes a poignant image of the peace that has been shattered prematurely.

The chapter begins by exploring Gene's numbed reaction to the consequences of his unthinking action in the tree. The leg, the doctor explains, is "shattered"—a term Gene cannot fully understand. And when the doctor also announces that "sports are over" for Finny, he assigns Gene the terrible responsibility to try to help his friend to come to terms with this devastating prospect. In no uncertain terms, then, Gene realizes that he has truly destroyed his friend—and not the imagined rivalry that he now sees as nothing more than his own selfish illusion.

Afraid of accusations and also frightened of his own deepest emotions, Gene retreats into himself, where he discovers paradoxically his own mirror image of his friend—and victim. Alone in the room he shares with Finny, Gene decides, on an impulse, to dress in his friend's clothes, including his pink shirt. In the mirror, Gene sees himself becoming Finny, even down to the expression on his face—"Phineas to the life."

Imaginatively restoring his friend to vigor, Gene feels momentarily relieved of his guilt—and at one with Finny. Yet this illusion, comforting as it is, lasts only a single night for Gene, although the theme of his identification with Finny—their doubleness, as it were—continues to develop throughout the novel.

Gene not only identifies with his friend, but also tries to confess his wrongdoing to Finny. Twice in the chapter, he makes the attempt, first at the infirmary and later at Finny's home in Boston, but both times the discussion ends without any true resolution. Yet even these attempted confessions show Gene struggling to cope with his psychological turmoil and still very much caught up in his conflicted emotions about Finny.

The scene at the infirmary—when he makes his first (abortive) attempt at confession—reveals the guilt, fear, and anger that Gene still feels toward Finny. Dreading a direct accusation, Gene hesitantly probes Finny's memory of the fall, hoping, it seems, to find a lapse of memory that would make his guilt disappear. When Finny remembers an urge to reach out and catch on to his friend, Gene reacts in anger and fear— "to drag me down, too!"—confusing his own unspoken violent impulses with Finny's simple and innocent instinct to save himself.

Theme

Reliving the fall with Finny in the infirmary room, Gene emphasizes his own pain and fear, insisting that the accident, in a sense, happened to him, too. Again, Gene seeks relief from his guilt through his identification with Finny.

As the two boys struggle with their memories, Gene tries to confess to Finny, but is interrupted by Dr. Stanpole. Actually, Gene welcomes the interruption, because he comes to his confession not so much out of contrition as shame. Indeed, before Gene begins his stuttering admission, Finny makes a confession of his own—he vaguely suspects that Gene somehow caused the fall—but quickly apologizes to his friend for thinking badly of him without any proof of wrongdoing. Ironically, then, it is Finny who confesses out of innocence—he feels guilty for guessing the truth—rather than Gene, who should be confessing out of guilt.

Character Insight

Gene's second attempt at confession takes place during an impulsive visit he makes to the recuperating Finny at his home outside Boston. His impulse here suggests the beginning of his growing maturity and personal integrity, which prompts his need to confess.

Yet, visiting at Finny's home, Gene feels like a "wild man." In fact, he launches into a declaration that seems more like another attack on Finny than an admission of guilt or a heartfelt apology. Finny, in turn, lashes out in anger, hurt by his friend's words and unable to accept the dark secret inherent in their meaning. And Gene, in turn, sees this reaction as a vindication of his own violent instinct; if Finny can express such murderous rage, Gene reasons, then his own action must be no worse than his friend's.

The truth of the matter, it seems, cannot really be discussed between the roommates. Uncomfortable but still wanting to be friends, Gene and Finny part on a false note—Gene will not lapse back into the old rules when he returns for the new term at Devon.

But Gene ends the chapter by foreshadowing his regression back into conformity when he judges this promise to be "the biggest lie of all."

Chapter 6

Summary

In this chapter, Gene returns to Devon for the Winter Session and notices immediately that the freedom of the summer days has come to an end. The ordinary business of the school term as well as changes due to the war now dictate life on campus, creating an atmosphere that is both serious and rigid.

As Gene hurries to report as new assistant manager at the Crew House, he thinks of Phineas' trick of balancing on a canoe and then tumbling headlong into the water. The thought pleases Gene, because it brings back the carefree image of his friend before his accident.

Gene meets Cliff Quackenbush, the crew manager, who treats him with contempt. Disgusted by Gene's inexperience and lack of motivation, Quackenbush calls him "maimed"—a remark that prompts Gene to hit Quackenbush in the face. In the struggle that follows, both boys end up in the water, and a drenched Gene leaves for his dormitory.

On the way to his room, Gene meets Mr. Ludsbury, a strict Devon master who warns him that the wild antics of the summer will not be tolerated any longer. Saddened by this stern lecture, Gene is only mildly curious when Mr. Ludsbury tells him he has a long-distance phone call.

It turns out to be Phineas on the phone, calling from home. In a friendly conversation, Finny again dismisses Gene's confession and expresses relief that they will still be roommates. The only conflict arises when Gene tells Finny about going out for assistant crew manager, a position usually taken by younger students with no athletic talents.

Outraged that Gene would even consider such a position, Finny tells his friend that he must go out for sports. Since Finny can no longer compete, Gene must take his place. With this pronouncement, Gene feels as if he is becoming part of Finny.

Commentary

This chapter emphasizes the changes in Devon and in Gene now that the Summer Session is over—brought to a close, symbolically, by

Finny's fall. The chapter begins with Finny's absence, but ends with him not only reasserting his presence, but also his influence over Gene.

Without Finny, Gene notices, peace seems to have "deserted Devon." The "gypsy days" of summer are gone, replaced by the "duration" of the war, and now Gene sees authority reasserting itself—as in the chapel sermon, for example—and demanding hardship and sacrifice.

The "gypsy music" of the summer has also vanished, replaced by the drone of duty and tradition. Note especially the title of the hymn, "Dear Lord and Father of Mankind, Forgive Our Foolish Ways"—an outright apology, it seems, for all the fun the boys had during the Summer Session.

Within this atmosphere, Gene cannot help but feel responsibility for his part in Finny's fall. In this chapter, he begins to understand his world more deeply as he struggles with the consequences of his inner turmoil—and his own darker self.

Water symbolism runs through the novel, and here it helps to dramatize Gene's sense of loss in the wake of Finny's fall. As narrator, Gene uses the metaphor of the two rivers flowing on either side of Devon to express the dual nature of the school as a protected, isolated community and also as a place connected directly to the world at war. It also symbolizes the sense of innocence and evil that Gene must come to understand and accept.

The fresh-water Devon River suggests the idyllic nature of the school—the sense of it as a kind of Eden. The river, where the boys have played all summer, runs through familiar farms and woods, its banks alive with pine and birch trees. Indeed, the river, flowing clear and unpolluted, symbolizes the freedom and innocence of the summer's "gypsy days."

Gene associates this river with Finny, who seems "like a river god." When Gene looks upon the Devon, he especially remembers Finny's spectacular balancing act on the prow of a canoe—his body poised effortlessly between the river and the sky—capped by his comic (rather than tragic) fall into the clear water.

But the Devon also flows into the Naguamsett River, whose murkier course suggests the darker instincts Gene must finally acknowledge as he moves toward an understanding of himself. In contrast to the Devon, the Naguamsett joins the ocean, making it subject to the tides and larger natural forces; its banks are marshy and muddy, its water salty.

The central scene of the chapter occurs here on the Naguamsett and contrasts sharply with Gene's happy memories of summer on the Devon with Finny. Without Finny, Gene withdraws into himself and in a half-hearted attempt at sports decides to become the assistant crew manager. Accordingly, he reports to Cliff Quackenbush, the sullen and humorless crew manager—a kind of anti-Finny, who presides over the boathouse and the river with a jealous spitefulness. Indeed, Quackenbush seems to be a nasty river troll rather than Finny's river god.

Character Insight

Unpopular and even actively disliked by other boys, Quackenbush sees Gene, his new assistant, as someone to whom he can finally feel superior—someone he can treat with utter contempt. For his part, Gene feels a kind of sympathy for the mean-spirited Quackenbush—a compassion that emerges from his own sense of guilty sinfulness after causing Finny's fall.

While Gene endures the crew manager's condescension and rejection, his pity evaporates when Quackenbush refers to him as a "maimed son-of-a-bitch." Clearly, Quackenbush here touches a sore point with Gene, who feels spiritually crippled for having maimed Finny. And so Gene strikes out at Quackenbush.

Gene's fury rises not only from his sense of being revealed by Quackenbush—he is, after all, morally maimed—but also out of his strong connection to Finny, who is, in fact, physically disabled from the fall. Once again, Gene instinctively identifies with Finny, transforming his guilt into shared pain.

Literary Device

The result of the fight between Gene and Quackenbush—a fall into the salty Naguamsett—represents a dirty dunking that contrasts sharply with the cleansing baptism of the Devon. While the earlier jump from the tree into the Devon opens Gene's eyes to a fresh vision of the world, this fall into the Naguamsett awakens him to a keener sense of his own guilt. Later, in the next chapter, Gene comes to accept his dunking as another kind of "baptism."

Theme

Gene's fall into the river also gains in moral significance when Mr. Ludsbury confronts him on the way to the dormitory. Gene's excuse—tellingly, "I slipped"—becomes the basis for Mr. Ludsbury's long and caustic sermon on the boys' disobedience during the Summer Session. Gene has "slipped" from Devon traditions and standards, according to the master, but he has also slipped morally from friendship through his own jealous spite. Dirty with salt and slime here, Gene appears as a fallen, filthy friend, unworthy of Finny's trust and regard.

This image of Gene contrasts sharply with the warmth and trust evident in Finny's unexpected phone call. The boys' friendship seems renewed on both sides—passively, on Gene's part, because he has not got a new roommate; and actively, on Finny's part, through his assertion of faith in Gene after their argument in Boston. But the moment of unity quickly yields to a study in contrasts and the reassertion of Finny's influence over Gene when the conversation turns to sports. As Finny tells Gene: "Listen, pal, if *I* can't play sports, *you're* going to play them for me."

This command represents both a challenge and a relief to Gene. Upon hearing Finny's wish, Gene becomes virtually one with the friend he has both idealized and destroyed. And it is in this moment that a sense of freedom suddenly sweeps over Gene, when he thinks about what his secret purpose must have been in jouncing the limb—"to become a part of Phineas."

Glossary

duration   the time that a thing continues or lasts. Here, a specialized term from World War II meaning "for as long as the war continues." For example, the maids at Devon will be gone "for the Duration," or as long as the war lasts.

Chapter 7

Summary

This chapter opens when Brinker Hadley, a leader of the senior class, visits Gene in his room. Brinker teases Gene about having a room to himself, suggesting that Gene has "fixed it" that way on purpose. Gene laughs off the remark uneasily, feeling as if Brinker is hinting that he deliberately caused Finny's accident.

Later in the basement Butt Room where students gather to smoke, Brinker pushes Gene into a crowd of boys and openly accuses him of "doing away with his roommate." In response, Gene makes up a long, silly list of crimes he committed against Finny, stopping short of actually admitting to his part in the fall. At this point, he dares a younger boy to guess what happened at the tree. When the boy answers that Gene pushed Finny off the limb, Gene tells him he is wrong and brushes him aside, exposing the younger boy to the ridicule of the others. Making an excuse about having to study, Gene escapes the awkward situation.

As the winter approaches, Devon students start to take on the work usually done by men now in the service. For a few days, the boys pick apples. Later, with the first heavy snow, they volunteer to dig out the railroad yards so that trains can pass. Only Leper stays behind, to ski through the countryside and take photographs.

The work on the railroad exhausts the boys, and the sight of the first train to pass—a troop train carrying young recruits—makes the students feel childish. Talk turns to training programs and recruitment—activities much more meaningful, they decide, than school. When Quackenbush insists that he will stay at Devon the whole year, the others sneer at him and question his patriotism.

As the returning students reach the school grounds, Leper appears, delighted with his day's skiing and proud of the photographs he has shot of a beaver dam. Protective of his friend, Gene congratulates him, but Brinker barely contains his annoyance. When they are alone, Brinker declares impulsively to Gene that he is going to enlist immediately.

Excited by Brinker's sudden decision and determined to face the challenge of the war himself, Gene bounds up to his room. But when he opens the door, he finds that Finny is back, and the plans about enlisting suddenly fade away.

Commentary

As this chapter opens, Brinker Hadley emerges as a possible new influence on Gene, in the absence of Finny who continues to recover at home from his accident. Like Finny, Brinker impresses Gene from the beginning as a well-liked and charismatic leader in the school, able to command attention and compliance with his interests of the moment.

Character Insight

But, unlike the independent Finny, Brinker comes by his leadership through conventional—even traditional—means. While Finny leads the boys in unofficial blitzball and the forbidden challenges of the Suicide Society, Brinker serves as the duly elected president of the Golden Fleece Debating Society. Unlike Finny, who seems almost unconscious of his effect on others, Brinker takes his leadership very seriously and campaigns constantly to maintain it.

After his baptism in the Naguamsett, Gene senses in Brinker a possible friend, but also a psychological inquisitor. Relentlessly, Brinker needles Gene about Finny, apparently recognizing dark motives behind the accident. When Gene tries to escape Brinker's insinuations, their psychological drama simply moves to the more public forum of the Butt Room.

Literary Device

In the Butt Room, a kind of kangaroo court unfolds, with the curious students as jury and Brinker as prosecutor, foreshadowing the more formal procedure (in Chapter 11) at the Assembly Room. And like Gene's earlier fight with Quackenbush on the Naguamsett, the encounter in the Butt Room—"this dungeon nightmare," as he calls it—unexpectedly touches Gene's worst fears about his true nature.

The charges Brinker levels against Gene in the Butt Room—"rankest treachery," "practically fratricide"—strike directly at his fear of being accused of causing Finny's accident. Suddenly Gene stands as "prisoner," with the scene of his crime openly identified—"that *funereal* tree by the river."

When one boy attacks with the bluntness of raw curiosity, Gene defends himself with ironic humor—silly confessions to serious crimes—but he cannot make himself joke about his part in Finny's fall. In this moment, Gene does try to admit his crime—as an absurdity, to disguise his guilt—but his throat tightens and words fail him.

Gene cannot yet truly acknowledge his guilt to others—or even, really, to himself, despite his earlier attempts to confess to Finny. Gene's guilt remains as a part of his deepest nature, and it will re-emerge in a more serious trial later in the novel—a trial that neither he nor Finny can escape.

After the mock trial in the Butt Room, the focus of the chapter turns to the war as winter comes to Devon. As part of the war effort, the school boys join in apple-picking—humorously celebrated in Brinker's Keatsian "Apple Ode"—and take up shovels against the heavy New England snow on the nearby railroad tracks.

The description of the railroad scene—grimy, run-down, industrial—creates a clear contrast with the sheltered Devon campus and the idyllic apple orchard. Here, at last, the boys play their part in a larger, rougher world, closer to the war and their own adulthood. They work all day under the sullen supervision of a railroad man—who seems an older version of Quackenbush—performing heavy labor with a real purpose.

Yet, when the tracks are cleared and the first train pulls through, the Devon volunteers again feel themselves returning to boyishness. The train carries young men barely older than the students, recruits who are off to the real war, leaving the Devon boys behind. The recruits' new uniforms, their excitement, the fact that they are going off to the war, make Gene and the other school boys feel even more isolated, more inconsequential, and, finally, childish.

Against this backdrop, Leper appears—the boy who consistently refused to jump from the tree and who has also skipped the shoveling to ski by himself. Here, in this chapter, Leper's eccentric interests, his isolation, and his vulnerability all become apparent, especially in contrast to Gene and Brinker.

Leper's appearance in this chapter also foreshadows later developments in the novel. For example, as Leper approaches Gene and Brinker, his touring skis move with the slow regularity of a piston engine—an image that will reappear later in his testimony (in Chapter 11) about Finny's fall from the tree.

This scene also dramatizes Leper's status as a loner at Devon. While the other boys battle winter with shovels, Leper keeps his own vigil in the wild, observing how animals dig into their homes to escape the harsh conditions. Leper's winter day, in fact, foreshadows his later inability to adapt to military life and his frightened retreat to his own snowy Vermont home after his nervous breakdown.

Leper's isolated calm contrasts sharply with Brinker's energetic instincts for action. Leper's announcement that he has found the beaver dam, and even has photographs, so infuriates Brinker that he is determined to enlist at once. Ironically, though, it is Leper, rather than Brinker or Gene, who will be the first from their class to enlist in the war.

When Gene, inspired by Brinker's sudden decision, thinks about enlisting, his vision of the future remains unclear—more a school boy's dream than a resolve to take up arms. It expresses itself in the arresting image of the blue and white weave of his school clothes cut off sharply by military shears and replaced by new khaki threads, woven in a new, unknown design. The thrill of the unknown, the challenge of adventure, rise in Gene here, even as he tries to think about the deadly danger of war.

His friendship with Finny, after all, is deadly—and the fall has brought an end to peace at Devon, at least for him, anyway. So, under a starry sky that seems to sharpen his resolve, Gene is determined to face the moment as the war demands.

But when he opens his door, Gene suddenly finds Finny returned to Devon in good spirits, though with a heavily bandaged leg. Gene's "crisis" of choice about the war and his role in it evaporates as he faces his friend.

All of Gene's imaginative energy focused on the future now disappears before the present reality of Finny, who represents the essence of vibrant life. And so a life force confronts Gene just as he has decided on a course of action—military enlistment—dedicated to killing.

Gene realizes in this final scene of the chapter, then, that Finny—rather than the war—will be his testing ground, his field of honor, his moment of life and death.

Glossary

butt the remaining end of anything; stub; stump; specifically the stub of a smoked cigarette or cigar. Here, the term is a slang word for cigarette, applied to the place where the boys at Devon gather to smoke, the Butt Room.

contretemps (French) an inopportune happening causing confusion or embarrrassment; awkward mishap. Here, Gene uses the word to play down the seriousness of Finny's fall.

fratricide the act of killing one's own brother or sister. Here, Brinker's characterization of Gene's doing away with Finny.

Golden Fleece (Greek Mythology) the fleece of gold that hung in a sacred grove at Colchis guarded by a dragon until taken away by Jason and the Argonauts. Here, the term is used as the name of the Devon debating society, emphasizing the club's exclusive quality, unconnected to reality.

interned detained or confined (foreign persons, ships, etc.) as during a war. Here, confined in prison for the war, the fate of many Japanese-Americans. When the boys question Quackenbush's loyalty, they wonder why he has not been confined as an enemy alien.

Mussolini (1883–1945) Benito Mussolini, Italian dictator, Fascist prime minister of Italy (1922–43), executed; called *Il Duce*. Here, someone questioning Quackenbush's loyalty asks if he intends to join Mussolini's army, the enemy of the Allies.

Kraut (slang) a German or person of German ancestry; a derogatory term.

Pearl Harbor inlet on the southern coast of Oahu, Hawaii, near Honolulu; the site of the United States naval base bombed by Japan on December 7, 1941. Here, the reference to the base denotes the entrance of the United States into World War II.

Abominable Snowman a large, hairy, man-like creature reputed to live in the Himalayas; also called yeti. Here, Leper in his ski gear reminds Brinker of the creature.

Chapter 8

Summary

As the chapter opens, Finny teases Gene and complains about the lack of maid service in the dormitories. When Gene says that the inconvenience is minor, considering the war, Finny murmurs his doubts about whether there really is a war at all.

The next morning, as Finny bounds around the room on crutches, Brinker comes by to ask Gene if he is ready to go enlist. When Finny is shocked by this, Gene suddenly changes his mind and jokingly refuses to sign up with Brinker. In the teasing that follows, Brinker receives his first nickname at Devon—"Yellow Peril."

Gene worries that Finny will fall again, because the snow and ice outside and the marble floors inside make it difficult for him to get around campus on crutches. Finny decides to miss class and go to the gym instead, a long and exhausting walk for him. Gene realizes that Finny's natural athlete's way of walking will never return, and Finny in turn tells Gene that he must become an athlete in his place.

Finny also tells Gene there is no war really—only fat old men pretending that it exists to punish young people who might have fun otherwise. These old men have faked the food shortage, too, Finny insists, so that all the best food can be shipped to the rich men's exclusive clubs. When Gene asks how he knows about this deception, Finny blurts out bitterly that he knows because he has suffered. He confides to Gene that he once hoped to compete in the Olympics, but now Gene will have to take his place in the 1944 Games. When Gene brings up the war, Finny reminds him that there is no war.

The boys begin a strict routine, with Gene helping Finny in his studies and Finny training Gene for the Olympics. One day, as he runs a challenging course laid out by Finny, Gene finds, to his surprise, that he can push himself beyond exhaustion to a second wind.

When Mr. Ludsbury comes out to ask Gene if he is training to become a commando, Finny proudly declares that they are aiming for the 1944 Olympics. Mr. Ludsbury laughs briefly, but sternly remind them that the war is more important than any games. Finny responds flatly, "no"—an answer that catches Mr. Ludsbury by surprise and sends him on his way.

Finny wonders why the master believes the lie about the war, and then it comes to him—Mr. Ludsbury is thin, and only the fat old men know the secret about the war.

Commentary

Theme

Peace has returned to Devon with Finny, and Gene's plans for enlistment vanish, almost without a thought. Finny's presence—especially his obvious injury—takes up Gene's entire reality, even the reality of his own future. From now on, Gene responds to Finny's needs, and enlistment, under such circumstances, seems to be desertion of Finny.

But choosing to stay at Devon rather than enlist means saying no to Brinker, a painful rejection that will have consequences later in the Assembly Room "trial." Brinker's needling about Gene's plot to get rid of his roommate is an obvious attempt to keep Gene and Finny's friendship from re-forming. But their caustic wit against Brinker expresses their renewed partnership, despite his "catastrophic joke."

When they mock Brinker together, they define their own friendship against him, reforging their union by excluding the popular leader. Their scorn for Brinker and his plans for enlistment represent a claim for their own shared future. Later, this scorn will turn back on Gene and Finny, though, when Brinker lays a claim on their murky, shared past at the tree.

The boys join together again, but the weeks apart have clearly changed them. Gene has become overly serious—even sanctimonious—about the hardships of wartime, while Finny's frame of mind, his expectations about daily life, remain firmly fixed in peace. At first, Finny's irreverence and flippancy about the war shocks Gene, but soon Finny draws Gene back under his influence, and before long, their relationship of leader and follower re-emerges, even in matters of war and peace.

Literary Device

Water imagery again surrounds the drama between the two friends. At the very mention of enlistment, for example, Finny announces that he is going to the shower, as if to wash away the thought of war and separation. And Finny's influence buoys Gene up, allowing him to ride the imaginative waves of wartime as easily as Finny rode the waves during their forbidden trip to the beach. At this point, the war itself, Gene decides in retrospect, swept over him "like a wave at the seashore," leaving him "peaceably treading water."

On his first day back at Devon, Finny cuts class and sets off for the gym—a long and difficult walk on crutches that foreshadows the later moment outside the Assembly Room when he slips and falls. As they walk to the gym, Gene becomes aware of the icy paths and the danger they pose for Finny on his crutches. And, as they move indoors, Gene also notes the floors and stairs—"smooth, slick marble, more treacherous even than the icy walks."

Appropriately, the gym, once the site of Finny's athletic triumphs, now becomes the forum for his most inspired flights of imagination—his twin fantasies about the fake war and the 1944 Olympics. With these two fantasies, Finny reasserts his leadership through imaginative rather than physical means. Injured, but not broken, Finny draws Gene into a new vision of the world in order to recreate Gene as his own double.

Finny's eccentric view of the war contrasts sharply with Gene's dutiful, olive-drab consciousness of wartime America. While Gene sees the dullness of disappointment and suffering—homesick young servicemen coming and going on trains that are never on time—Finny imagines a vast conspiracy of fat old men frustrated by their own incapacity and embittered by the possibility of other people having fun.

While Gene's view calls upon its believers to sacrifice, Finny's incites rebellion. Finny's vision assumes a real war between generations behind the fake war between nations—a fabricated rumor that enables the old to keep power, wealth, and pleasure to themselves. Given the fake war, sacrifice is meaningless.

Instead of sacrifice, Finny's vision demands amused detachment, a refusal to give one's heart or mind to the cause trumpeted by a lying older generation. In such a world vision, Gene and Finny are essentially on their own, with only each other to trust.

Finny's fake war theory attacks the dominant world view, but his vision of the 1944 Olympics proposes a new world altogether. As Gene points out, an Olympics two years away—in 1944—would be impossible, because the war will almost certainly still be raging, and so prevent a peaceful form of competition between nations. But if there is no war, as Finny maintains, then the 1944 Olympics is virtually a reality already for the athletes training for it. Finny's 1944 Olympics, then, represents an anti-war, a reality that must be accepted in light of the fake war.

When Finny invites Gene to train for the Olympics in his place, he invites him, in essence, to join him in a new world—to become, in fact, a part of him. The invitation—the challenge, really—to Gene grows out of an uncharacteristic moment for Finny, a sullen mood created by his weeks of suffering. But Gene's deliberate effort at chinning the bar rouses Finny, re-creating his unique spirit even in adversity. Clearly, the collaboration of trainer and athlete will benefit both: Finny will relive his lost glory through Gene, while Gene will grow in unexpected ways through reforging his close bond to Finny.

Finny's carefully planned track for Gene's run circles a "patriarchal elm tree"—a site recalling the fatal tree by the river. In fact, the training for the imaginary Olympics takes a form that recalls the boys' challenging play on the river the previous summer.

But this time, in winter, the boys have switched places, with Finny passively resting on the tree and Gene energetically throwing himself into action. Here Finny merely watches while Gene pushes himself beyond his limits, finding the second wind that makes the exertion a joy rather than a test of endurance.

Instinctively, Gene realizes that the experience makes him more like Finny. Once overly conscious of Finny's extra ten pounds, Gene now feels as if his friend has grown smaller, or, perhaps, that Gene has "all at once grown bigger."

Perhaps Gene has become Finny's double at last—a true twin, rather than one simply dressed in his clothes. The resolution of the rivalry might be the happy ending of another story, but not this novel. In the chapters ahead, the boys' relationship will meet other challenges, and Gene will again face the reality of his guilt.

Glossary

Bunyan Paul Bunyan, the giant lumberjack of American legend.

Elliott Roosevelt the son of Franklin Delano Roosevelt (1882–1945), 32d president of the United States. Here, Gene refuses to enlist with Brinker, even if he were the son of the president. In turn,

Brinker claims a family connection with the wealthy, powerful Roosevelts.

the Eton playing fields observation "Eton" town in Buckinghamshire, on the Thames, near London; site of a private preparatory school for boys. Here, Mr Ludsbury refers to the phrase used by the Duke of Wellington (1769–1852). In the Duke's opinion, the Battle of Waterloo, in which the British defeated the French led by Napoleon, was won "on the playing fields of Eton," the result of the spirit of the British officers who first learned to compete in the vigorous games of their schools, notably the prestigious Eton.

General MacArthur Douglas MacArthur (1880–1964), United States general, commander in chief of the Allied troops in the southwest Pacific during World War II.

Guadalcanal largest island of the Solomon Islands in the southwest Pacific. Here, the site of an United States victory after a long, bloody struggle (1942–43).

gull a person easily cheated or tricked. Here, Gene offers Leper as an example.

Madame Chiang Kai-Shek (Soon Mei-Ling) the wife of Chiang Kai-Shek (1888–1975), Chinese generalissimo and head of the Nationalist government on Taiwan (1950–75). Here, a reference to the couple's representation of wartime China in international circles.

Prohibition the forbidding by law of the manufacture, transportation, and sale of alcoholic beverages. Here, Finny is referring to the period between 1920 and 1933 when the sale of all alcoholic beverages was forbidden by an amendment of the United States Constitution.

Yellow Peril the threat to Western civilization presented by Asian people, especially those of China or Japan; widely believed in during the late 19th and early 20th centuries in North America, Europe, and Australia. Here, Finny gives Brinker the nickname when Gene says he is really Madame Chiang Kai-Shek.

Chapter 9

Summary

The chapter opens with the enlistment of Leper Lepellier, who decides to join the ski troops. The first recruit from the class, Leper simply makes up his mind and goes quietly, without any fanfare. Brinker begins to connect any triumphal news of the war with Leper, and the Devon students imagine their former classmate—at least in their jokes—as a war hero.

Only Finny refuses to imagine Leper as a legend. When he sees that talk in the Butt Room always revolves around Leper's imaginary heroism, Finny forbids Gene to go there, on the grounds that smoking is bad for athletes. Gene finds himself isolated from the rest of school life, alone with Finny in a world where the 1944 Olympic Games seem more real that World War II.

To liven up a dull winter, Finny invents the Devon Winter Carnival, an event that takes place on the banks of the Naguamsett River and includes sports, snow statues, food, and music. Finny presides over the action, which includes a ski jump, a prize table, and jugs of hard cider, guarded by Brinker. At the signal, Chet Douglass blows his trumpet, and the boys attack Brinker to raid the hard cider. In the midst of the riot, Gene pours cider down Brinker's throat, and Brinker declares the Games open.

Finny, however, objects. He officially opens the Games with "the sacred fire from Olympus"—a copy of the *Iliad* doused with cider and set ablaze. The boys, excited by the cider, throw themselves into the games, while Finny, atop the prize table, dances on one leg. Gene surpasses himself athletically, freed by the Carnival's imaginative escape from the realities of war.

When a telegram arrives for Gene, Finny grabs it, announcing it must be from the Olympic Committee. But, instead, the telegram is from Leper, who explains that he has escaped and needs Gene to come to him immediately—"at Christmas location."

Commentary

Theme

As this chapter opens, Gene explains that his own happiness, rather than a belief in Finny's conspiracy theory, created a kind of peace for him during that winter when the rest of the world was at war. This theme of a personal sense of peace—the "separate peace" of the title—will reach its climax with Finny's Winter Carnival.

Even Leper's sudden enlistment seems not to affect the separate peace of Devon—at least for a while. When Leper watches a war recruitment film, he becomes dazzled by the angelic images of soldiers skiing across the virgin snow. Once a dedicated, slow-moving "touring" skier, Leper now longs to speed downhill, despite the danger. In fact, he changes his mind not only about the war, but about skiing, too, drawing the connection between sports and war that Finny has been fighting for months.

When Leper enlists as the first volunteer from Devon, he disappears, almost without a word, into the world of war. The silence surrounding Leper's leave-taking and the lack of information about his part in the war encourages wildly imaginative tales that Brinker weaves into the Leper legend. The hapless Leper, Brinker jokes, must be the hero behind all the victories the Devon boys read about in the papers—a kind of ubiquitous Kilroy.

Character Insight

Only Finny—who refuses to acknowledge the war, anyway—does not join in celebrating the Leper legend. In contrast to Brinker's sarcastic mock-sagas of the Devon hero, Finny makes his own spontaneous plans for the Winter Carnival, emphasizing energy and freedom—the creation of a new world apart from the world at war.

With the Carnival, Finny re-emerges as the spiritual leader he was during the Summer Session, making up rules according to his own whims. Indeed, he inspires the other boys—including the straitlaced Brinker—to organize the winter carnival in much the same rebellious way that he once organized the game of blitzball and the Super Suicide Society.

Literary Device

Significantly, though, the Winter Carnival takes place near the marshy Naguamsett, not the clear Devon of the summer. Even Finny's fun, it seems, is moving toward the outside world, like the salty Naguamsett that flows into the sea. Again, the water imagery makes poignantly clear the loss of Edenic isolation: The splendid Devon, so calm and clear, is no longer a place for the boys; instead, they now play near a river that will carry them inevitably to the sea, and adulthood.

Finny, it seems, can hold off the war—but only for a while.

Still, with the Carnival, he performs his magic once more, creating, through the sheer force of his personality, an afternoon of escape from the worries of the draft and enlistment, an imaginative refuge from the world at war. Appropriately, the Carnival opens with the ritual burning of Homer's *Iliad*—the poetic account of the Trojan War—as a gesture that represents the symbolic destruction of the idea of war itself.

With the Winter Carnival, Finny conjures up out of his magical concoction of cider, sport, and music, an alchemy of peace—his own imaginative version of the 1944 Olympics. In keeping with Finny's Olympic vision, Gene sees himself as the center of glory, crowned with a ceremonial wreath. For a moment, Gene even becomes the embodiment of Finny's athletic aspirations, imagining himself taking off from the ridiculously low ski jump and soaring in flight—"hurtling high and far through space."

The real highlight of the Carnival, though, comes with Finny, who climbs up on the prize table and dances on one leg, recreating his balancing act in the canoe from the summer on the Devon. Graceful even in injury, Finny seems once more, for this almost magical moment, a kind of god creating an imaginative world of his own, full of high spirits and joy, as he dances out a "choreography of peace."

When the outside world suddenly invades with the arrival of a telegram for Gene, Finny tries, imaginatively, to transform the telegram into Gene's invitation to the 1944 Olympics—the confirmation in reality of an enduring dream. But Gene himself opens the envelope, and any idea of the Olympics vanishes. The message, in fact, comes from Leper and urgently calls Gene to join him "at Christmas location"—an odd code name, whose very secretiveness seems to evoke the dangers of war.

As unavoidable and uncompromising as a draft notice, then, Leper's telegram brings the Winter Carnival to an end, taking Gene away from dreams of Olympic glory and Finny's world of peace.

Glossary

Archangel seaport in northwestern Russia, at the mouth of the Northern Dvina River. It is icebound for six months every year.

Burma Road "Burma," the old name for Myanmar, country in southeast Asia on the Indochinese peninsula. Here, the supply route for the Allies beginning in Burma and extending far into China, where American and Chinese troops fought the Japanese.

Big Three the leaders of the United States, Great Britain, and the Soviet Union, the most powerful Allied nations in World War II.

Bolsheviks originally, a member of a majority faction (*Bolsheviki*) of the Russian Social Democratic Workers' Party, which formed the Communist Party after seizing power in the 1917 Revolution. Here, Finny means the Soviet Union.

Free French inhabitants of the part of France and its colonies not invaded by Germany in 1940.

de Gaulle Charles de Gaulle (1890–1970), French general and statesman; president of France (1959–69). Here, the reference is to de Gaulle's leadership of the Free French during World War II.

Giraud Henri Honore Henri Honore Giraud (1879–1949), French general, de Gaulle's rival for leadership of the Free French.

Ruhr river in west central Germany, flowing west into the Rhine; major coal-mining and industrial region centered in the valley of this river. Here, it refers to the industrial region heavily bombed by the Allies in World War II.

Scharnhorst a German battleship torpedoed by British destroyers and then sunk by the battleship *Duke of York* in December, 1943.

Stalingrad old name of Volgograd, city in the south central part of the Soviet Union, scene of a decisive Soviet victory (1943) over German troops in World War II.

Tunisian campaign Tunisia is a country in north Africa, on the Mediterranean. The Tunisian campaign was the series of battles between the Allied forces and the combined German and Italian forces in North Africa (January to May, 1943).

Sad Sack (slang) a person who means well but is incompetent, ineffective, etc., and is consistently in trouble. Here, the kind of person Gene fears he might become under the pressure of combat.

Chapter 10

Summary

In this chapter, Gene travels by train to Leper's house. As he stops for coffee, he concludes that Leper's "escape" must have been from spies. The legend of Leper, created in fun at Devon, seems to have come true.

As Gene approaches the house, he notices Leper watching him from a window, not moving even as Gene stands at the front door. When Gene opens the door himself, Leper appears and ushers him into the dining room—the only place, he tells Gene, where "you never wonder what's going to happen."

When Gene jokes and lightly teases him, Leper's response is angry, then despairing. Leper has changed, Gene sees, and he begins to understand that his friend has become mentally unbalanced. The "escape," Leper explains, was from the Army and a section-eight discharge that would have labeled him a "psycho."

Laughing hysterically and shouting angrily, Leper tells Gene that his experience has revealed a lot to him about himself and others— especially the "savage underneath" that lurks in Gene. Suddenly, he accuses Gene of deliberately causing Finny's fall. In response, Gene rises angrily and kicks over Leper's chair. The noise brings Leper's mother, and Gene apologizes, saying he will leave, but Leper, still laughing, invites him to stay for lunch.

After the meal, they walk through the snow together, and Gene tries to talk to Leper calmly. The conversation breaks down when Leper begins sobbing uncontrollably, confessing that he is haunted by disturbing images, such as a man's face on a woman's body, or the arm of a chair coming to life as a human arm. When Leper tells these frightening details from his psychotic episode in the Army, Gene shouts at his friend to shut up and runs away.

Commentary

First and last, the journey to Leper is, for Gene, a journey within himself. This trip, which he takes without Finny, brings Gene face to face with a different and disturbing vision of himself—the "savage underneath."

Before recounting his visit to Leper's home in Vermont—the "Christmas location"—Gene (as adult narrator) offers an extended recollection of his wartime service, made up, he remembers, of many nighttime trips. After all the training and travelling, he explains, the war was nearly over, and so he never saw battle.

Ironically, then, Leper's telegram represents a kind of draft notice for Gene. In answering Leper's strange call, Gene experiences what the war will be for him—not terrifying combat, but long, dark journeys without a clear purpose.

Now, as he travels through the night, Gene thinks about Leper's telegram, wondering—in a fantasy that rivals Finny's conspiracy theory about the war—if his friend's "escape" is really from wartime spies. Even the description of the remote Vermont area where Leper lives—and has now retreated—emphasizes this sense of danger, with its bitter cold and wind, its snow and isolation. It is, to Gene's mind, a "death landscape."

As Gene trudges toward the Lepellier house, he spies Leper standing at the window—alone, intent, immobile, not moving even to open the door. While Leper once skied happily to explore how animals took shelter in winter, now he himself desperately seeks refuge, hiding in his dining room, as if he were one of the beavers he once sought to study.

Clearly, Gene's arrival invades Leper's uneasy world, but Leper also harbors a revelation that will shake Gene's own self-image and vision of the future. As a result, this chapter—the only one set entirely away from Devon—stands as a pivotal moment in the novel, because its drama sets in motion the action of the concluding three chapters as well as the tragic crisis of the story, which turns on Leper's reappearance at Devon.

The change in Leper, his alternating laughter and tears, makes clear that he has suffered a mental breakdown in the army. Agitated and defensive, Leper spits out the word he imagines Gene is thinking— "psycho."

As if the mere mention of this pseudo-clinical term frees him, Leper suddenly pours out a stream of frighteningly true observations about Gene himself. Leper declares that Gene pushed Finny out of the tree, because Gene is "a savage underneath."

Accused and judged, Gene responds to his own dark instincts, his secret impulses, and knocks Leper from his chair, just as he once pushed Finny from the tree. Again, in a moment of blind anger, Gene strikes out at a friend, and, in his fury, embodies the brute emotions at the heart of war.

Here, then, in a remote Vermont farmhouse, far from the action, war exists in Gene himself, as a confused burden of fear, anger, and blind impulse. As his earlier recollection makes clear, Gene will never see combat, but in Leper—and in his own reaction to Leper—he sees the consequences of war dramatized in psychological terms.

Leper's psychosis creeps outward, bringing on, in Gene, too, a crisis of identity. The confrontation, with its revelation about his nature, forces Gene to retreat into a comforting self-image, just as the emotionally wounded Leper has retreated to his home. Embarrassed, confused, Gene imagines Leper's protective mother judging him in flattering terms, despite his angry attack on her son—as "a good boy underneath," rather than "a savage underneath."

Later, on their walk together in the snow after lunch, Leper confides his delusions to Gene, and this conversation recalls the scene (in Chapter 9) when Finny reveals his vision of the fake war conspiracy to Gene. In both instances, Gene passively listens to a strange and surprising view of reality offered by a friend in crisis, but the contrast between these two scenes underscores the crucial difference between Finny and Leper.

The harrowing, close-up view of Leper's hallucinations suddenly makes Finny's unorthodox stories look normal and healthy in comparison.

Finny's vision may be unconventional, and perhaps even paranoid, but it enables him to move imaginatively in a world that he finds physically challenging because of his injury. The fake war theory represents Finny's active, rebellious involvement in the wider world.

But Leper's visions—like Snow White with Brinker's face—virtually paralyze him, and his other delusions—of men turning into women, the arm of a chair becoming a human limb—reduce him to hysteria.

Leper's perceptions of the real world behind the war are psychotic and destructive—not imaginative and creative, like Finny's.

Theme

Finally, the details of Leper's breakdown—the first reality of the war that might await the Devon boys—prove too much for Gene to take. In Chapter 9, Gene sits absorbed during Finny's rambling explanation of the fake war, and rises to the challenge of the dreamlike 1944 Olympics, but here he withdraws suddenly from the confiding Leper, shouting, "I don't care!"

The horrible vision of wartime psychosis, so close after Finny's separate peace of the Carnival, terrifies Gene, and he abandons his friend in the snow, fleeing him, literally, as he would a leper.

Chapter 11

Summary

Shaken by what he has learned about Leper, Gene returns to Devon, wanting to see Finny again. He finds him in the middle of a chaotic snowball fight, in which all the boys end up playfully attacking Finny. Gene worries that Finny may injure his leg again with such rough play, but Finny insists that he is careful and adds—to Gene's relief—that he can feel the bone growing stronger.

When Brinker visits the boys' room to ask about Leper, Gene answers that Leper is "Absent Without Leave." Finny assumes that Leper has grown tired of the army, but Brinker sees the truth at once, declaring that now two students from the class are out of the war, the second being the injured Finny. Gene resists this idea, resorting to Finny's notion that there is no war, but when Finny agrees with only a fading grin, Gene knows that he is being ironic.

One morning after chapel, Brinker tells Gene that his failure to enlist comes from pity for Finny. He also says that Gene should put the accident in the past by seeing all the details come to light. Brinker hints darkly that Gene knows what he means.

Working on a translation of Caesar's *Gallic Wars,* Gene and Finny discuss the current war. Finny admits that Leper's mental breakdown has convinced him of the reality of the war, and he tells Gene that he has even seen Leper at Devon. The boys decide not to tell anyone about Leper's presence.

Later, Brinker and other boys come to take Gene and Finny by force to the Assembly Room in the First Building. There Brinker formally opens an inquiry into the circumstances of Finny's accident to end any "stray rumors and suspicions." When Brinker questions him, Finny first recalls Gene at the bottom of the tree but then remembers that they climbed the tree together. This contradicts Gene's own false statement, and only Leper, who also witnessed the accident, can resolve the difference.

Leper appears and makes it clear in his own strange and mystical version of the event that Gene jounced the limb just before Finny fell.

When Brinker insists they must investigate further, Finny shouts him down and rushes out of the room in tears. The boys hear Finny's cane tapping and then the sound of him falling down the marble stairs.

Commentary

When Gene arrives back at Devon at the beginning of this chapter, he still reels from his shocking encounter with the mentally disturbed Leper. He seeks comfort in the familiar campus, but most of all he wants to see Finny—"and Phineas only."

He finds Finny in the midst of a snowball fight, child's play compared to the brutal adult reality of war that drives Leper "psycho." And while a blanket of snow covers both Devon and the Lepellier home in Vermont, the school campus seems to Gene to be innocent and Edenic, with the promise of an "untouched grove"—a sharp contrast to Leper's "death landscape."

The snowball fight, significantly, offers the last view of Finny at sports. It ranges chaotically, like blitzball, with little regard to anything but Finny's wild whims. And—in a foreshadowing of how Gene imagines his friend might behave in actual combat—Finny switches sides back and forth during the fight, betraying both teams for the sake of the disorderly game.

For Finny, Gene realizes, conflict always becomes play, a lively rather than a deadly rivalry. The thought comforts Gene, but shames him, too, in light of Leper's accusation. For Gene, it seems, even play can turn into war. Saddened by the revelation, Gene wants to find a separate peace again with Finny.

But that is no longer possible. With Gene's journey, the war comes to Devon, and the truth about Leper—as well as the truth Leper brings with him—inevitably emerges. Brinker, especially, senses the reality of Leper's situation. In a foreshadowing of his role in the Assembly Room trial, he asks a few leading questions, sifts through the facts, and comes to the harsh but true conclusion that Leper has "cracked up."

For Finny in particular, Leper's mental breakdown represents undeniable proof that the war exists. The news shatters his theory of a fake war and destroys the imaginative refuge that he once shared with Gene. Now, Finny confesses, he only believes in Gene—but his faith proves unfounded, making both of them vulnerable.

Suddenly, Brinker drags them off to a highly theatrical trial. The Assembly Room, where the trial is set, symbolically recalls Leper's "death landscape," with school boys somberly dressed in black robes, and the windows staring down on the proceedings with a "deadened look." Even Leper himself appears, finally, in a starring role.

Just as Finny once led the Suicide Society, Brinker now takes command, hoping to reprise his role as Gene's psychological inquisitor. In fact, he assumes that, under his careful examination, the emerging facts will resolve the question of Gene's guilt once and for all.

But the truth of the fall does not conform to Brinker's legalistic expectations. Finny's testimony, for example, emerges as a muddled mass of conflicting and false memories about Gene's position near (or in) the tree. At one point, Finny even suggests that the tree itself shook him from the limb—a strangely magical notion that would leave Gene entirely guiltless.

But Brinker perseveres in bringing legal clarity to this uncertain situation. Intrigued by Finny's conflicting memories and Gene's own inconsistencies, Brinker suggests that another witness to the fall—Leper—might clear up everything, if only he were at Devon.

When Finny turns to Gene—the only other person who knows that Leper is, in fact, at Devon—he clearly expects his friend to speak up and help him to resolve the mystery of his fall. But Gene, ashamed and frightened in the knowledge of his guilt, does nothing to bring Leper forward—leaving it to Finny instead.

Gene's silence amounts to yet another betrayal. In fact, it recalls the two previous instances when Gene said nothing in response to Finny—on the beach, and, most recently, during their discussion of Caesar and the Gallic War—and may, perhaps, even remind the reader of Peter's three denials of Christ.

When Leper arrives on the scene to testify, he takes the trial spinning off into the realm of hallucinatory revelation—and also truth. In his recounting of the fall, Leper offers a strangely mystical vision of light and darkness, in which two silhouetted figures appear on the limb "black as death." To this, Leper adds—in a strange echo of his own skiing style—that the figure nearest the trunk moved up and down "like a piston."

The recollection may be confused and fragmented, but the boys seize on one incontrovertible point—the boy who moved up and down made the other fall. As prosecutor, Brinker presses for details, but Finny rises in anger. Like Gene, he cannot bear the truth of Leper's disturbing reality.

With the same words that Gene screamed at Leper at end of the previous chapter—"I don't care!"—Finny now furiously charges from the room to the foyer, where he slips on the marble steps and falls, once again to be broken by Gene's disloyalty.

Glossary

Athens capital of Greece, in the southeastern part of the country; Athens became established as the center of Greek culture in the 5th century B.C., when it was the capital of ancient Attica. Here, a model for Devon.

Sparta ancient city of Laconia in the Peloponnesus, a peninsula forming the southern mainland of Greece. Here, a model for the representatives of various branches of the military.

Hitler Youth "Hitler" Adolf Hitler (1889–1945) Nazi dictator of Germany (1933–45), born in Austria. Here, the term refers to a Nazi program designed to promote discipline and loyalty in German children and adolescents. Finny uses it in his joking description of the free-for-all snowball fight.

LST the initials stand for "land ship tank"; a vessel designed to land large numbers of troops on a beach quickly.

Chapter 12

Summary

After Finny's second fall, Dr. Stanpole arrives to take charge. He tells Gene that Finny has broken his leg again, but that it appears to be a simpler fracture — "much cleaner" than the original injury.

Against orders, Gene follows the doctor's car taking Finny to the infirmary. There Gene spies through a window, calling to Finny. In fury, Finny struggles to rise from his bed but falls out of it instead. Apologizing, Gene leaves quickly, and spends the night wandering through the campus. Next morning he awakens in a corner of the ramp beneath the stadium.

Returning to his room, Gene finds a note from the doctor, asking him to bring clothes to Finny in the infirmary. He packs a suitcase and takes it to Finny, who speaks calmly but unpacks the clothes with trembling hands. Suddenly Finny slams his fist on the suitcase and tells Gene that he has been trying desperately to enlist in the military, but no one—not even the Canadians and Chinese—will take him because of his injury.

Gene tells Finny he would never have been any good in the war anyway, because he would have wanted to play baseball with the enemy instead of fighting. Brought to tears by this, Finny asks if Gene's part in the fall was just "blind impulse," and not a deliberate expression of hate. Gene assures him, and Finny gratefully accepts the explanation.

Gene spends the rest of the day in school activities, but returns to the infirmary at five o'clock to check on Finny after the surgery to set his leg. There he learns from Dr. Stanpole that marrow from the broken bone had leaked into the bloodstream during the operation and traveled to Finny's heart, killing him. Although he is overwhelmed by the news of Finny's death, Gene does not cry, not even at the funeral, because he feels as if it is actually his own funeral.

Commentary

The events following the second fall emphasize the separation between the roommates now that Finny knows Gene's responsibility in the original accident. While Finny can no longer believe in his friend, breaking the unity between the two boys, Gene, in turn, understands his guilt, and that knowledge nearly drives him crazy.

Literary Device

The night of the second fall, Gene suffers a kind of emotional breakdown that recalls Leper's hysterical hallucinations. For example, as Gene lurks outside the infirmary trying to see Finny, he resists an irrational impulse to steal the doctor's car. Later, when he spots Finny and the doctor inside the room, he imagines absurd conversations and weirdly comical remarks that bring him—like Leper in Vermont—to laughter and tears.

Later that night, Gene suffers from "double vision"—a kind of hallucination that also recalls Leper's breakdown. The gym, for example, seems familiar, yet "innately strange," a "totally unknown building" with a significance that Gene cannot fathom. The whole world, in fact—and especially the gym which he associates with Finny—seems apart from Gene, as if everything around him is real, but he is a dream.

Clearly, Gene's nightmare vision of himself comes from the knowledge of his guilt—and the separation that he now feels from Finny. Indeed, Gene fears that he no longer exists, and so can never be a part of Finny's world again. Even his attempt to visit Finny that night in the infirmary room seems to prove this beyond a doubt. Angry at the sight of Gene, Finny tumbles out of bed.

Even in good faith, it seems, Gene cannot help but cause Finny to fall. Yet, ironically, Gene now finally (if obliquely) offers Finny the apology he should have given in the summer—"I'm sorry, I'm sorry."

Like Leper, who must retreat into the delusional safety of his Vermont dining room, Gene seeks refuge for the rest of the night in the "sheltered" corner of a stadium ramp. On his way to the infirmary the next morning, Gene tries to regain his emotional balance by comparing his own "brief burst of animosity" with the enormous atrocities of war. But his rationalizations break down as he nears the room—and the reality of Finny.

Still, Gene's last conversation with Finny in the infirmary expresses all that has so far gone unspoken between them. In anguished disappointment, Finny confesses his efforts to enlist, and, in turn, Gene finally says the truth he feels about his friend—that Finny would be no good in the war, because his natural impulses point him always toward friendship and sports, not animosity and fighting.

This insight about Finny seems to have been hidden within Gene's consciousness throughout the novel, and only the open revelation of his own guilt—the truth about himself—can bring forth the truth about Finny. As Gene speaks the words, then, he knows their importance as the proof of his friendship—the expression of his deep understanding of Finny, and even his love for him.

Gene's admiration—and his total lack of hatred—challenges Finny to return the trust of his friend. The question about Gene's guilt has always gnawed at Finny, despite his reluctance to admit it, even to himself. Gene's two earlier attempts to admit his guilt ended badly, but now Gene's openness and vulnerability enables the subject to emerge fully, without defensiveness or anger.

Note that Finny does not ask: "Did you make me fall?" Leper's statement, after all, has already established that fact. Finny does not even ask: "Why did you make me fall?" Instead, he offers his trust, asking, in tears, whether Gene acted out of "some kind of blind impulse," rather than hatred.

Finny frames the question carefully as the offer of an explanation, not the demand for one. When Gene accepts it gratefully, adding his own admission of "some ignorance inside," the reconciliation restores the boys' unity.

And this unity survives even Finny's death. Doctor Stanpole broods over his responsibility as the attending physician, but it is Gene, finally, who understands the meaning behind Finny's unexpected death, caused by the marrow from his leg traveling fatally to his heart. The broken leg has, in effect, broken Finny's heart, and so Gene senses his own responsibility for his friend's death.

Yet, even as he grieves for Finny, Gene does not cry, because he feels as if he himself is dead. Since he is now at one with Finny, Gene feels as if a fundamental part of himself has died with his friend.

Glossary

"Gallia est omnis divisa in partes tres"   Latin phrase meaning "Gaul is divided into three parts;" the beginning of Caesar's *Gallic Wars*.

Chapter 13

Summary

As the last chapter opens, the war has come to Devon in the form of the Parachute Riggers' School. The School occupies the Far Common, with jeeps, trucks, and sewing machines.

Gene goes with Brinker to the Butt Room, where they have a talk about military service with Mr. Hadley, Brinker's father. Mr. Hadley sneers at the soldiers learning to sew and cheerily asks Gene which branch of service he prefers. Gene explains that he is planning to join the Navy in order to avoid being drafted into the infantry, while Brinker, too, has made a careful choice, deciding on the relative safety of the Coast Guard. This disgusts Mr. Hadley, who urges them to think about how their military service will sound when they talk about it in the future. The safest choice may not be the wisest choice in the long run, he explains.

Afterward, Brinker complains of his father's hearty enthusiasm for war service, especially since the older generation will not face any risk in the war that Brinker insists they caused. Brinker's thinking reminds Gene of Finny's theory about the fake-war conspiracy of "fat old men." But for himself, Gene decides that the war arose from something "ignorant" within humanity itself.

As Gene empties his locker to leave Devon for military service, he thinks of Finny and their friendship, which still remains a vital part of his life. Later, from his adult perspective, Gene believes that his war actually ended before he ever entered military service. He sees now that he killed his "enemy" at Devon, while Finny, always unique, never saw anyone or anything as his enemy.

Commentary

Theme

After Finny's death, war (and the conspiracy Finny envisioned behind it) come finally to Devon. But Gene has learned from Finny, and from Finny's death, to take both in stride. The final chapter makes clear that Gene is ready to enter the wider world of the war and his own adulthood.

The arrival of a military unit at Devon is almost comic in its understatement, as months of sermons about high-risk service culminate in the headmaster's welcoming a Parachute Riggers' School—soldiers armed with sewing machines rather than machine guns. Still, the regulation uniforms, the maneuvers, the strident voice of the commander, form a sharp contrast with the scholarly, New England surroundings. Devon and the military really are meeting now, and the clash underscores the fact that the boys will be going off to war soon.

Ironically, the mission of the unit seems ideal—although a little late—for the tragedy that has occurred at Devon. Parachute riggers, after all, work to make falls safe for young men. The outcome of Finny's fall emphasizes the importance of their job, despite the domestic connotations of the sewing machines. The vision of thousands of Finnies falling to the ground and surviving brings an unexpectedly optimistic angle on the war.

Character Insight

Mr. Hadley, Brinker's father, also arrives, representing in his pink-cheeked "portliness" the fat and foolish old men that Finny once imagined as the conspirators of the fake war. Appropriately for the flesh and blood model of the boy's fantasy, Mr. Hadley speaks on only one subject—war service—and his remarks make clear that he sees young men as either adventurers—like him—or else worthless cowards. The insensitivity of his talk, his condescending bullying of Gene and Brinker, gives a human voice to Finny's fat old men in their stuffy clubs.

Mr. Hadley sees himself differently, of course. He proudly stands on his World War I experience—which is sketchy, according to his son—and advises the boys to choose a high-risk service, to ensure an impressive collection of stories to tell. For Mr. Hadley, the reality of war rises to its greatest importance years afterwards, in competitive talks with other men. He urges his son toward dangerous war service, therefore, just as he would advise him to choose a prestigious college, to ensure respect and position in later years. In effect, for him, a man's war service becomes his resume.

Theme

Gene's response to Mr. Hadley dramatizes how the acceptance of his own guilt has made him more accepting of others' weaknesses. Brinker's resentment of his father rises from his anger at the older generation who caused the war but now face no threat from it. But Gene views Brinker's father with less anger, and even some compassion. In fact, unlike Brinker or Finny, Gene does not blame the war on the older generation, but on "something ignorant in the human heart"—the same incomprehensible feeling that prompted him to jounce the limb and make Finny fall.

The conclusion makes clear that Gene acknowledges both his guilt in Finny's death and Finny's enduring power in his life. At Devon, Gene recalls, "I killed my enemy"—the uncertain, angry self that caused Finny's accident. Drained of fury and fear, Gene accepts the challenge of service and lives through the war without the burden of hatred, falling into conventional military step "as well as my nature, Phineas-filled, would allow."

In his life and death, then, Finny gives Gene a part of his own vital spirit—a natural gift for friendship, humor, and peaceful harmony—that sees his friend through the war that awaits him, and adulthood, too.

Glossary

doughboys United States infantrymen, especially of World War I. Here, Brinker's father uses the word to describe the World War II recruits he sees at Devon.

foxhole a hole dug in the ground as a temporary protection for one or two soldiers against enemy gunfire or tanks. Here, it represents the infantry fighting Gene hopes to avoid.

Maginot Line (after A. Maginot [1877–1932], French minister of war), a system of heavy fortifications built before World War II on the eastern frontier of France; it failed to prevent invasion by the Nazi armies. Here, Gene uses the term to describe the barriers people put up to defend themselves against a perceived threat.

CHARACTER ANALYSES

Gene Forrester 64

Phineas (Finny) .65

Brinker Hadley 66

Elwin (Leper) Lepellier 67

Gene Forrester

Gene serves as both the narrator and protagonist in the novel. Telling the story from his perspective, he recounts his own growth into adulthood—a struggle to face and acknowledge his fundamental nature and to learn from a single impulsive act that irrevocably shapes his life.

Gene's name suggests what he might be—but is not. In an ideal matching of gentility with hardiness, "Eugene" means "well born," while "Forrester" suggests natural independence and outdoor resourcefulness. Yet Gene seems neither particularly noble nor physically impressive; his character, in fact, finds its definition in his limitations and his fundamental reserve, rather than his accomplishments.

As a southerner, Gene feels like a stranger in a northern landscape. Attending an elite New England boarding school, he tries to romanticize and inflate his background by hanging pictures of plantations on his wall, hoping to impress fellow students as a southern aristocrat.

A solid but not a brilliant student who succeeds through discipline, obedience, and conventional thinking, Gene at once admires and envies Finny, his roommate, for whom athletic—if not scholastic—success comes so easily. Gene must work hard for everything he attains, and so he resents the ease of Finny's physical ability and the graceful spontaneity with which he engages life.

By his very nature, Gene conforms and embraces the conventional. In contrast to Finny, he wants to follow the rules—spoken and unspoken—as if in a kind of lock-step. His "West Point stride," for example, suggests this tendency toward conformity—even, potentially, the military conformity that looms before all the boys at Devon.

With tragic consequences, Gene's conformity brings him into conflict with rebellious Finny, but his natural reserve prevents him from expressing his feelings openly and directly. As a result, Gene's anger churns within him and emerges in unconscious forms—a "bending of the knees," for instance, that shakes the limb of the tree at the critical moment and causes Finny to fall.

Yet, as much as Gene resents Finny's freedom, he needs him to become a complete human being. Over the course of the story, Gene functions as Finny's opposite—but he also becomes his double. At the end of the novel, Gene gratefully accepts the forgiveness of his friend, whose death he mourns in silence, as he readies himself to face the world without resentment or fear.

Phineas (Finny)

Finny is the only character in the novel for whom Knowles does not provide a last name. Unlike Gene Forrester, whose name offers two different meanings (well-born and hardy), Finny's character needs no qualification: Finny is just Finny.

True to his aquatic-sounding name, Finny lives in action like a fish in water—moving, playing, challenging others to join him. Finny's game of blitzball, for example, expresses his essential nature with its spontaneous style of play and its rules made up on the run.

For all of his immediacy, though, Finny appears to the reader only from Gene's perspective. As narrator, Gene shares his own feelings while observing Finny's actions and speech, but he never enters his friend's thoughts. For example, Gene (and the reader) learns only late in the novel that Finny desperately wants to enlist in the military—*any* military—and that his fantasy about the fake war simply represents a way of hiding his pain.

Because Gene focuses so much on Finny, Finny himself assumes a paradoxical role in the story—neither narrator nor protagonist, yet still clearly central to the novel. And while most fictional characters come alive because they change over the course of the story, Finny's vitality emerges instead from the fact that he remains the same—his fundamental characteristics consistent from beginning to end.

From his clothes—especially that pink shirt—to his daring jumps from the tree, Finny flouts all the prep school conventions as the classic rebel in an overwhelmingly conformist world. Yet Finny's actions—even his most dangerous antics—spring up spontaneously, out of a natural enjoyment of life, without a trace of deviousness or vindictiveness, and this innocence informs his view of everyone else as well. Finny, for example, cannot imagine that Gene might envy him his easy success as an athlete, nor does he suspect that his friend's secret animosity might suddenly erupt in violence.

As the innocent in this story of Eden lost through human weakness and war, Finny emerges finally as a kind of Christ-like figure. Through the sacrifice of his suffering and death, Finny redeems Gene, offering his friend—in their essential doubleness—the promise of a better self.

Brinker Hadley

Brinker plays a secondary role in the novel as Gene's inquisitor before and during the Assembly Room trial. His public performance in the Assembly Room represents his most dramatic moment; aggressive, but scrupulously polite, he pursues responsibility irresponsibly.

A successful, conventional student leader, Brinker stands in contrast to both Finny (the unconventional leader) and Gene (the unquestioning follower). Smooth and carefully dressed, Brinker strives to impress people and, when he can, exercise control over them.

The glimpse of Brinker's father in the last chapter throws some light on Brinker's character. The son of an overbearing father, Brinker develops his aggressive tendencies in self-defense; he manipulates and bullies people to avoid being manipulated or bullied himself.

In fact, Brinker uses his manipulative powers to compete with Finny for Gene's loyalty. Brinker senses Gene's dark secret—that he envies and resents Finny—and tries to exploit it by needling him about his friend. Brinker's manipulation takes an especially cruel turn as he escalates his needling into the trial in the Assembly Room. Here his motivation seems strangely similar to Gene's own in causing Finny to fall. Indeed, as the story dramatizes, affection—and even love—can become harmful and finally destructive in the emotionally charged atmosphere of a boys' prep school.

By the last chapter, Brinker seems less aggressively competitive—but, of course, Finny is dead now, and the competition is over. Brinker actually comes around to profess a version of Finny's conspiracy theory about the war and even produces a chief example in the person of his own father, who seems to be one of those fat and foolish old men behind the war.

Yet Brinker seems less mature in the last chapter than Gene, who can now view Mr. Hadley with tolerance and even pity. In fact, Brinker functions here as a kind of measure by which the reader can gauge Gene's growth toward adulthood after he comes to terms with Finny's death and his own culpability.

Elwin (Leper) Lepellier

Leper is another important minor character in the novel. In fact, he acts as a kind of narrative catalyst, inadvertently bringing about the final tragedy in the novel.

The nonconforming loner Leper serves as a contrast to Finny, another nonconformist who nonetheless succeeds as a leader. Quiet and shy, Leper is most comfortable by himself exploring the world on his own terms, as he does when he skis to the beaver dam.

From the beginning, Leper breaks down under stress. Challenged by Finny to jump from the tree, he freezes. Tossed the ball in blitzball, he refuses it. And, faced with the rigors of basic training, he suffers a mental breakdown—thus becoming a "psycho," who runs away from the army.

Leper's breakdown distorts his reason but it also sharpens his insight, as his accusatory remarks to Gene make clear in chapter set in Vermont. When the usually unassuming Leper returns to Devon, he also manifests a power that even Brinker cannot control in the Assembly Room trial. In fact, as he testifies under Brinker's questioning, Leper sees the underlying truth of Finny's fall in apocalyptically prophetic terms—and the consequences, of course, prove tragic.

CRITICAL ESSAYS

From Innocence to Experience 69

Gene and Finny: Doubles 71

From Innocence to Experience

A Separate Peace tells the story of Gene's painful but necessary growth into adulthood, a journey of deepening understanding about his responsibility and his place in a wider world. At the beginning of the novel, the young Gene stands unconcerned, self-absorbed, by the tree that will test his true nature. By the end, Gene has suffered and inflicted suffering, and he has grown into an understanding of his own dark motives. He has lost his innocence and has gained experience.

Gene's innocence at the opening of the novel represents a childlike happiness in conformity. By obeying the rules—occasionally rebelling mildly through sarcasm, "the protest of people who are weak"—Gene maintains a comfortable life, predictable and unthreatening, like Leper's dining room. In Devon, obedient to the rules, approved by the masters, Gene is safe, but he cannot grow. Growth can come only through conflict and struggle, and Gene's conformity acts as a shield against such challenges.

Finny breaks through Gene's shield of conformity, daring him to experience the world more directly, by breaking rules and creating new traditions. With Finny, Gene explores a life unbounded by familiar routines imposed by adults. The freedom exhilarates Gene at times—the first forbidden jump from the tree brings him to a new, heightened awareness of life—but uncertainty nags at him. Finny's whims disturb Gene's comfortable routine of study and proper behavior, habits of obedience that win the approval of adults.

Frightened and threatened by Finny's freedom, Gene reacts like a child—sullen, withdrawn, indirect in expressing objection. Instead of joining Finny wholeheartedly or honestly talking through his feelings (about studying for exams, for instance), Gene suppresses his mixed emotions and turns the new experience of freedom into another kind of conformity: He decides that he must follow Finny's whims without exception or risk losing his friendship. This "all or nothing" thinking, childish in its simplicity, leads Gene to resent Finny and ultimately causes the violent outbreak that destroys a life.

Out of Gene's discomfort arises a dark suspicion: Finny is deliberately drawing Gene away from his studies in order to make him fail. Psychologically, this makes sense to Gene. If Gene is trying to obey the rules in order to win approval—the only validation he really recognizes—then anyone who encourages him to disobey, or follow other rules, must wish him harm. Finny, therefore, must be his enemy. In his own defense, Gene hides his resentment and lets his (seemingly justified) anger burn within him while he single-mindedly pursues his goal to become the best student and so show up Finny.

But Gene's sudden recognition that Finny does not want him to fail proves even more devastating. If Finny is simply being Finny in his free, careless ways, then Gene has lost the meaning of his resentment, the energy that has been fueling his drive to succeed despite his enemy's plotting. Gene's anger and bitterness toward his friend make sense only if Finny is really a lying, manipulating enemy bent on destroying Gene. And Gene's quest for academic excellence makes sense only as means of showing up Finny.

The realization that Finny is not acting as a rival or an enemy, but simply as himself, makes Gene feel insignificant. Like a child who discovers he is not the center of the universe, Gene rages at the insult. On the limb, beside his friend, Gene acts instinctively, unconsciously, and expresses his anger physically by jouncing the limb, causing Finny to fall. The physical release of emotional tension suddenly frees Gene, and he jumps effortlessly, without fear, as he never could before. With the destruction of the threat, Gene's view of the world, and of himself, is restored. The child's self-image of himself as the center of the world is recreated.

Significantly, in describing his actions on the limb, Gene insists not that he bent his knees, but that his knees bent, as if his body were not under his control. Again, Gene takes shelter in a childish, self-centered defense. I did not do it, Gene seems to be saying, my knees did it.

A fall and a tree sharply recall the story of Eden, the Fall of Man, and with it the end of innocence. With Finny's fall, Gene recognizes in himself what Leper condemns as "the savage underneath," the tragic flaw Finny more kindly refers to as "a blind instinct." Gene's sense of guilt, however much he hides it, represents his first pang of morality that needs no outside confirmation. Gene knows what he did, and he knows that he is guilty. For the first time, Gene's sense of right and wrong comes not from bells or exams or masters, but from his own shocked soul. This is the end of innocence, and the beginning of experience for Gene.

But faced with this self-knowledge, Gene rejects it, defensively retreating into his habitual conformity, his comforting sense of himself as an obedient boy. What starts out as a confession and an apology to

Finny—a mark of true growth into adulthood and responsibility—quickly becomes an angry rationalization, an attack on Finny that constitutes a second injury. In Brinker's informal Butt Room trial, and later, in the more formal Assembly Room investigation into Finny's accident, Gene persists in withholding the truth, refusing to admit his responsibility. Gene's resistance to the truth is a resistance to growth, a retreat into his passive, conforming past, where he felt safe and good. The revelation of Gene's guilt and his refusal to admit it cause Finny's second fall, the accident that ultimately ends his life.

Only in the friends' last conversation, in the infirmary, can Gene face Finny and freely discuss the fall on Finny's own terms, without rationalization or duplicity. Gene's apology and Finny's forgiveness make it possible for Gene to break out of his self-centered denial. By the end of the novel, Gene has accepted both his own guilt and the gift of Finny's friendship. The experience has helped him to grow into an insightful, responsible, and compassionate adult.

Gene and Finny: Doubles

Shortly after Finny's fall from the tree, Gene, consumed by guilt and fear, obeys a strange compulsion to dress like his roommate. He puts on Finny's clothes—even the unconventional pink shirt that was the "emblem" for the Allied bombing of Central Europe—and looks at himself in the mirror. There Gene sees he has become Finny "to the life." The physical resemblance Gene senses, brings on a surge of Finny's own unique spirit within him. Unexpectedly, Gene feels free, daring, confident—just like Finny. For a moment, Gene has become Finny's double.

In a sense, Gene and Finny have been each other's doubles since the beginning of the novel. In the first description of the boys standing together by the tree, the narrator makes clear that they resemble each other physically to a remarkable extent. Their heights and weights are nearly identical, although Finny weighs about ten pounds more than Gene. But the crucial ten pounds, Gene notes with envy, are distributed evenly over Finny's body. Finny, therefore, does not look like Gene with extra weight. Instead, next to Gene, Finny's entire physique looks more filled out, somehow more striking. This weight difference, "galling" to Gene, seems to prove that Finny stands as the larger, more substantial, somehow more generous, of the two. For Gene, then, Finny represents another version of himself, only better and more powerful.

Without even trying, Finny shows Gene up in the most basic, physical way. Even more frustrating, Finny accepts his shorter than average height without difficulty, while the unconfident Gene tries to embellish his own physical stature by adding a half-inch. When Finny hears this, he virtually cuts Gene down to size by attesting flatly that they are the same height. Gene cannot lie about himself, it seems, because his other self—as like him as his shadow—will speak the truth.

The "shadow" side of the double expresses Gene's mixed feelings about Finny from the start. Some critics have identified Finny as Gene's "Doppelganger," another self, wild and uncontrollable, that Gene loves but feels he must destroy. Gene is the good boy, the theory explains, the student who wants to obey, but is prevented by dark forces beyond his control, represented by Finny.

Throughout the novel, Gene's preference for an orderly life is disrupted by Finny's whims, impulsive and dangerous. As much as Gene enjoys these occasional thrills, he feels threatened—both academically and personally—by Finny's freedom. At one point, Gene even becomes convinced that Finny's outings and forbidden jaunts are a deliberate attempt to sabotage Gene's plans to become the valedictorian. Since Gene's academic ambitions are so close to his heart, so crucial a part of his self-image, the suspicion horrifies and angers him.

Given this tension, Gene's instinctive jouncing of the limb might represent a kind of self-defense: an unconscious attempt to destroy, or at least to cripple, a dangerous, uncontrollable part of himself—his shadow self. Gene's action, then, takes away Finny's power to disrupt Gene's orderly progress towards conventional adulthood. After the fall, Gene does not have to fear the consequences of Finny's unthinking action. The irony, of course, is that Gene's own unthinking action will have terrible consequences of its own.

As one a scholar and the other an athlete, Gene and Finny have been complementary selves—their abilities completing each other in friendship. After the fall, Finny determines to make the union of selves real in Gene, by training him to excel in sports as well as academics. For a superb athlete like Finny, the loss of physical ability represents an essential loss of self, a pain expressed in his uncharacteristically bitter remark, "I've suffered!" Yet Finny trains Gene with grace and good humor, delighting in his physical progress, generously sharing the dream of the 1944 Olympics. In fact, Finny trains Gene as enthusiastically as if Gene were a part of himself. Gene feels Finny's identification, and responds in turn by becoming, in his own way, a part of Finny.

The dramatic revelation of Gene's part in Finny's fall breaks the friendship temporarily, bringing about a nightmarish loss of self in Gene, but their reunion makes possible a new, more complete life. After Finny's death, Gene senses a new peace in himself, a self-confidence that enables him to cope with minor annoyances, like the condescension of Brinker's father, as well as great challenges, like service in the war.

By the end of the novel, Gene has fulfilled the earlier promise of the image in the mirror. He has killed his "enemy"—a narrow, fearful self—and filled himself with Finny's self-confidence and freedom. Gene has become a bigger and better self through friendship with his uncontrollable, unpredictable double, Finny.

CliffsNotes Review

Use this CliffsNotes Review to test your understanding of the original text and reinforce what you've learned in this book. After you work through the essay questions, identify the quote section, and the fun and useful practice projects, you're well on your way to understanding a comprehensive and meaningful interpretation of *A Separate Peace*.

Identify the Quote

1. "Well," I replied in a stronger voice, "first I stole all his money. Then I found that he cheated on his entrance test to Devon, and I blackmailed his parents about that, then I made love to his sister in Mr. Ludsbury's study, then I . . . ."

2. "The fat old men who don't want us crowding them out of their jobs. They've made it all up."

3. "They'd get you some place at the front and there'd be a lull in the fighting, and the next thing anyone knew you'd be over with the Germans or the Japs, asking if they'd like to field a baseball team against our side."

4. "I owed it to myself to meet this crisis in my life when I chose, and I chose now."

Answers: (1) [In the Butt Room, during the kangaroo court assembled by Brinker, Gene tried to joke about the accusation that he deliberately pushed Finny out of the tree to have the dorm room to himself. Gene finds he can't say "I pushed him."] (2) [In the gym, the injured Finny tells Gene his theory of the fake war conspiracy.] (3) [In the infirmary after the second fall, Gene tells Finny that his lack of hatred would disqualify him for combat.] (4) [After Brinker announces his intention to enlist, Gene decides to enlist also. His mind is changed within minutes, when he finds that Finny has returned to Devon.]

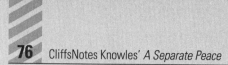

Essay Questions

1. On the beach, Finny calls Gene his "best pal," but Gene cannot respond in the same way. At this point in the novel, how is Finny a "best pal" to Gene? How is Gene not a "best pal" to Finny? Do the friends' feelings about each other change as the novel progresses? Explain your answers with references to the novel.

2. The tree by the river strongly recalls the Tree in the Garden of Eden, the site of original sin. Three different characters offer their own ideas about Gene's moral guilt in making Finny fall. Leper accuses Gene of being always "a savage underneath," Finny talks about "some kind of blind impulse," and Gene confesses to "some ignorance inside me." What do each of these descriptions mean? Which do you think is closest to the truth? Defend your answer with evidence from the novel.

3. The two rivers, the Devon and the Naguamsett, play important roles symbolically in the novel. What does each river tell us about Devon? How does Knowles use the rivers to make his point about innocence and experience? Why is it important that the Devon runs into the Naguamsett and the Naguamsett runs into the sea?

4. Leper's delusions are clearly the product of his psychosis. Yet when he describes the events at the tree in his testimony, he seems to be telling the truth in a kind of poetry. Discuss the images and poetic symbols Leper uses in his testimony about Finny's fall. What does Leper's poetic testimony tell us about this tragic event?

5. Leper's mother and Brinker's father are the only parents who actually appear in the novel. What does the character of each parent tell about that parent's son? If both parents represent the older generation, what conflict exists between the generations?

6. Like Gene, Brinker grows over the course of the novel. Discuss Brinker's changing views of Gene, the war, enlistment, and responsibility. How does the Brinker who first appears at Gene's door become the Brinker who prepares to leave Devon with Gene in the last chapter?

7. Finny's views on the war include great contradictions, from his wearing of the pink shirt as an emblem, to his conspiracy theory, to his letter to Chiang Kai-Shek proposing to join the Chinese army. What does Finny really think of the war? Do his feelings change over the course of the novel? If so, how and why?

Practice Projects

1. Create a Web site to introduce *A Separate Peace* to other readers. Design pages to intrigue and inform your audience and invite other readers to post their thoughts and responses to their reading of the novel.

2. Choose a scene from the novel and dramatize it for other classes. The production will require putting the scene in play form (freely adapting according to inspiration), assigning roles, directing, and staging the production. Follow the performance with a discussion of the novel's themes.

3. For a creative writing assignment, imagine Brinker's visit to Devon after 15 years. What places would he visit? What particular events would he recall? How would his time at Devon have affected the rest of his life?

4. Go to the library or news archives to research newspaper articles about the World War II battles and events mentioned in the novel. How was the war progressing during the Summer Session of 1942 and the following Winter Session? Discuss what effect the news might have on boys in school during this time.

CliffsNotes Resource Center

The learning doesn't need to stop here. CliffsNotes Resource Center shows you the best of the best—links to the best information in print and online about the author and/or related works. And don't think that this is all we've prepared for you; we've put all kinds of pertinent information at www.cliffsnotes.com. Look for all the terrific resources at your favorite bookstore or local library and on the Internet. When you're online, make your first stop www.cliffsnotes.com where you'll find more incredibly useful information about *A Separate Peace*.

Books

This CliffsNotes book, published by IDG Books Worldwide, Inc., provides a meaningful interpretation of *A Separate Peace*. If you are looking for information about the author and/or related works, check out these other publications:

A Separate Peace: The War Within, by Hallman Bell Bryant, analyzes the characters, themes, and images of the novel. Also includes useful information about the life and career of John Knowles. Part of the Twayne's Masterwork Studies series. Boston: G.K. Hall, 1990.

Lord of the Flies, by William Golding, explores many of the same themes as *A Separate Peace*, including innocence and experience, the growth from adolescence, and the tension between individuality and conventionality in the modern world. New York: Capricorn Books, 1959.

Peace Breaks Out, by John Knowles, is a later novel also set at Devon. Useful for comparison of themes and characterization. Also provides interesting contrast of the author's early and later writing. New York: Holt, 1981.

The Catcher in the Rye, by J.D. Salinger, is another novel of adolescence, featuring a prep school boy struggling to make sense of his life. New York: Little, Brown, 1951.

Like a Brother, Like a Lover, by George-Michael Sarotte, discusses Gene's confused feelings about Finny as an expression of unacknowledged love. The author argues that Gene's anger towards Finny comes from a fear of falling in love with his friend. Garden City, New York: Doubleday, 1978.

The Sporting Myth and the American Experience: Studies in Contemporary American Fiction, by Willey Lee Umphlett, analyzes Finny in comparison to characters identified with sports in other novels. Lewisburg, Pennsylvania: Bucknell University Press, 1975

It's easy to find books published by IDG Books Worldwide, Inc. and other publishers. You'll find them in your favorite bookstores (on the Internet and at a store near you). We also have three web sites that you can use to read about all the books we publish:

- www.cliffsnotes.com

- www.dummies.com

- www.idgbooks.com

Internet

Check out these Web resources for more information about John Knowles and related works.

A Separate Peace **Home Page,** www.exeter.edu/ library1/separate_ peace/index.html—features Knowles' reflections on his novel and Exeter, a photo essay on Exeter sites used in the fiction, the first page from the original manuscript. The site also offers articles from the wartime *Exeter Bulletin*, discussing the special summer session and preparations for war.

Author Spotlight, www.mcdougallittell.com/lit/ guest/knowles/ index.htm—a concise presentation of the life and literary works of John Knowles. Contains links to other authors, novels, and language arts subjects.

Next time you're on the Internet, don't forget to drop by www.cliffsnotes.com. We created an online Resource Center that you can use today, tomorrow, and beyond.

Films and Other Recordings

GISENAN, NANCY. *A Separate Peace.* San Francisco, Dramatic Publishing, 1968. A stage adaptation of the novel.

A Separate Peace, Paramount, 1972. A feature film based on the novel and the stage adaptation.

Journals

KNOWLES, JOHN. "My Separate Peace." Esquire March, 1985: 106–09. The author's own recollections of the writing of the novel.

KNOWLES, JOHN. "On *A Separate Peace,*" *The Exonian* November, 1972: 2. Knowles' thoughts on the novel, shared with other alumni of Philips Exeter Academy.

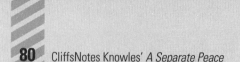

ROSENFIELD, CLAIRE. "The Shadow Within: The Conscious and Unconscious Use of the Double." *Daedalus: Journal of the American Academy of Arts and Sciences* 92 (1963): 12–15. The author identifies Finny as Gene's rule-breaking double, a frightening figure that he feels he must destroy. An early, influential study of the novel.

Send Us Your Favorite Tips

In your quest for learning, have you ever experienced that sublime moment when you figure out a trick that saves time or trouble? Perhaps you realized you were taking ten steps to accomplish something that could have taken two. Or you found a little-known workaround that gets great results. If you've discovered a useful tip that helped you understand *A Separate Peace* more effectively and you'd like to share it, the CliffsNotes staff would love to hear from you. Go to our Web site at www.cliffsnotes.com and click the Talk to Us button. If we select your tip, we may publish it as part of CliffsNotes Daily, our exciting, free e-mail newsletter. To find out more or to subscribe to a newsletter, go to www.cliffsnotes.com on the Web.

Index

A

Abominable Snowman, 38
academics, Finny's attitude toward, 24
accusations of Gene's guilt, 48, 50
aide-memoire, defined, 25
anger, 29, 50
apology to Finny, Gene's, 57
Archangel, 46
Assembly Room (symbolism), 54
Athens, 55
athletic prowess, Finny's, 20

B

baptism, 32
betrayal, 54, 55
Big Three, defined, 47
blind anger, 50
blind impulse, 56, 58, 70
blitzball, 19–21, 65
blitzkrieg, 21, 22
Bolsheviks, 47
Brinker
    character analysis, 66
    compared with Gene, 66
    contrasted to Finny, 35
    desire to enlist, 37
    influence on Gene, 35
    questions to Gene (foreshadowing), 53
    summarized, 8
    teasing Gene, 34, 40
    understanding of Leper, 52, 53
    Yellow Peril, 39
Bunyan (Paul), 42
Burma Road, 47
Butt Room, 34, 35, 38

C

Chiang Kai-Shek, Madame, 43
Churchill, Winston, 22
confession of guilt, Gene's, 28, 29
conflict vs. play, 53, 56
conformity as a shield, 69
conformity vs. individuality, 5, 6

contempt, 32
contrasts between Gene and Finny
    conflict vs. play, 20, 21
    conformity vs. individuality, 6, 22, 64
    eccentric vs. realistic, 41
    hurt blindly vs. help instinctly, 25
    maturation vs. childishness, 16
    spite vs. trust, 33
    thoughtful vs. unconcerned, 14
contretemps, defined, 38
crew manager, assistant, 30, 32

D

de Gaulle (Charles), 47
death of Finny, 56
death, understanding, 58
Devon River (symbolism), 31
Devon Winter Carnival, 44–46
disregard for authority, Finny's, 21
doughboys, defined, 62
draft, the military, vs. enlistment, 5
duration, defined, 33

E

enemy, 60, 62
enlistment
    allure of, 34, 37
    Brinker's, 7
    choices, 60
    Leper's, 44, 45
    the military draft vs., 5
envy. See resentment by Gene against Finny
Eton playing fields observation, 43

F

fall down the marble staircase, Finny's,
    55, 56
fall from the tree, Finny's, 23, 25, 31
fear, 14
fearful sites, 12, 13, 25
Finny. See also contrasts between Gene and
    Finny. See also influence of Finny on
    Gene
    anarchy, 20
    athletic prowess, 20
    attitude toward academics, 24
    broken leg, 58
    careless peace, 16

Finny, *(continued)*
    changed theory on the War, 52, 53
    character analysis, 65
    confiding in Gene, 19
    conflict vs. play, 53, 56
    consequences of fall from the tree, 28
    conspiracy theory on the War, 39–41, 50,
        61, 65
    death of, 56
    disregard for authority, 21
    early theory about the War, 15, 17
    fall down the marble staircase, 55, 56
    fall from the tree, 23, 25, 31
    fantasies, 41
    individualism, 6
    influence on other boys, 45
    influence over Gene, 17
    innocence, 20, 21, 24, 29, 65
    Lazarus and, 24, 26
    play vs. conflict, 53, 56
    recovery from his fall from the tree, 27
    shattered leg, 28
    spontaneity, 16, 19, 65
    summarized, 8
    symbolism, 16
    true sport, 21
first jump from tree limb, Gene and
    Finny's, 12
foreshadowing
    blitzball's maneuvers, 21
    Brinker's questions to Gene, 53
    Gene's loss of balance on tree limb, 17
    Leper's appearance carrying skis, 36
    Leper's ski outing, 37
    physical struggle, 14
    snowball fight, 53
forgiveness, 58, 64, 71
Forrester, Gene. *See also* resentment by Gene
    against Finny. *See also* contrasts between
    Gene and Finny. *See also* influence of
    Finny on Gene
    admiration toward Finny, 58
    apology to Finny, 57, 71
    betrayal against Finny, 54, 55
    character analysis, 64
    confession of guilt, 28, 29
    conflict vs. play, 53
    consequences of Finny's fall from the
        tree, 28
    contrasted to Brinker, 66
    fall into Naguamsett River, 33
    hallucinations, 57
    hysteria, 57

    identifying with Finny, 28, 30, 32, 64,
        71–73
    impressions on revisiting Devon, 13
    inability to confide in Finny, 19
    influenced by Brinker, 35
    journey to see Leper, 49
    maimed morally, 32
    play vs. conflict, 53
    significance of his first and last names, 64
    summarized, 8
    telegram from Leper, 46, 49
foxhole, defined, 62
fratricide, defined, 38
Free French, 47
friendship and blind anger, 50

G

Gallia est omnis divisa in partes tres,
    defined, 59
Gandhi, 25
Garden of Eden, 14, 17, 24, 53, 70
Gene. *See* Forrester, Gene
Giraud, Henri Honore, 47
Golden Fleece Debating Society, 35
Golden Fleece, summarized, 38
gratitude, 18
grayness (symbolism), 23, 24
Guadalcanal, 43
guilt, 7, 29
gull, defined, 43
gypsy days of summer, 31

H

Hadley, Brinker. *See* Brinker
Hadley, Mr., 8, 61
Hitler Youth, 55

I

ignorance, 58, 60, 62
Iliad, 46
individuality vs. conformity, 5, 6
influence of Finny on Gene
    enlist, to not, 37, 40
    Leper legend, about the, 44
    mixed feelings, creating, 14, 18
    peaceful harmony, of, 62
    play sports, to, 33
    spontaneous, to be, 16
    War, about the, 41

innocence, 53, 69, 70. *See also* Finny:
    innocence
inspiration, 7
interned, defined, 38
irony, 61

J

jealousy. *See* resentment by Gene against
    Finny
jump from tree limb, Gene and Finny's
    first, 12

K

Knowles, John (author)
    awards, 3
    Double Vision, American Thoughts from
        Abroad (novel), 3
    Hartford Courant (newspaper), 2
    Holiday (magazine), 2
    Indian Summer (novel), 3
    Morning in Antibes (novel), 3
    Paragon, The (novel), 3
    Peace Breaks Out (novel), 2, 3
    Phillips Exeter Academy, 2
    Phineas (short story), 3
    Private Life of Axie Reed, The (novel), 3
    Spreading Fires (novel), 3
    Stolen Past, A (novel), 3
    Vein of Riches, A (novel), 3
    Yale University, 2, 3
Kraut, defined, 38

L

Latham, Phil, 9
Lepellier, Elwin. *See* Leper
Lepellier's Refusal, 21
Leper, 14, 51
    accusations of Gene's guilt, 48, 50
    appearance carrying skis
        (foreshadowing), 36
    character analysis, 67
    character development, 34, 36, 37
    enlistment of, 44, 45
    legend of, 44, 45
    mental breakdown of, 48–50
    opinions about the War, 50
    ski outing (foreshadowing), 37
    Suicide Society, 23, 24
    summarized, 8
    telegram to Gene, 46, 49

LST, defined, 55
Ludsbury, Mr., 9, 30, 32, 39, 40

M

MacArthur, General (Douglas), 43
Maginot Line, 62
Mahatma, defined, 25
marble staircase, 13, 53, 55
maturation, 69, 71, 73
mock trial, 7, 35, 36, 52–54
mud (symbolism), 13
Mussolini, 38

N

Naguamsett River (symbolism), 31, 32, 45
Ne Plus Ultra, defined, 26

O

Olympics, 7, 39–42, 46
original sin, 17

P

Parachute Riggers' School, 60, 61
Patch-Withers, Mr., 15, 16
patriarchal elm tree (symbolism), 42
peace, personal sense of, 45, 62
Pearl Harbor, 38
Peter's three denials of Christ, 54
Phineas. *See* Finny
physical struggle (foreshadowing), 14
pink shirt (symbolism), 15, 16
pivotal moment in plot, 49
play vs. conflict, 53, 56
powerlessness, 9
Prohibition, 43
Prud'homme, Mr., 9, 15

Q

Quackenbush, Cliff, 30, 32, 34

R

railroad, boys' work on, 34, 36
reconciliation, 8, 56, 58
recovery from his fall from the tree,
    Finny's, 27
recruits on the train (symbolism), 36

redemption, 65
refuge, 49, 57
resentment by Gene against Finny
  end of, 8
  imaginativeness, about, 16, 17
  playing vs. working, about, 7, 64, 69, 70
  power Finny has over Gene, about, 14
rivalry, 23–25, 28
role reversal, 25
Roosevelt, Elliott, 43
Ruhr (River), 47

S

sacrifice, 41
Sad Sack, defined, 47
savage underneath, 48–50, 70
Scharnhorst, 47
school swimming records, 19
shame, 29
shattered leg, Finny's (symbolism), 28
silence as betrayal, 54
snowball fight, 53, 55
Sparta, 55
staircase, marble, 13, 53, 55
Stalin, Josef, 22
Stalingrad, 47
Stanpole, Dr., 9, 27, 56, 58
Suicide Society, 7, 15, 20, 23, 24
swimming records, school, 19
symbolism. *See also* tree by the river
  Assembly Room, 54
  blitzball, 20
  Devon River, 31
  Finny, 16
  Finny's broken leg, 58
  Finny's fall from the tree, 31
  Finny's shattered leg, 28
  Gene's fall into Naguamsett River, 32
  Gene's journey to see Leper, 49
  grayness, 23, 24
  loss of balance on tree limb, 17
  marble staircase, 13, 53
  mud, 13

Naguamsett River, 31, 45
Olympics, 42
parachute riggers, 61
patriarchal elm tree, 42
pink shirt, 15, 16
snowball fight, 53
Suicide Society, 20
telegram from Leper, 49
train of recruits, 36
unity of a single day, 23
water, 31, 41, 45

T

telegram from Leper, 46, 49
train of recruits (symbolism), 36
transition from present to past, 14
tree by the river
  changed by time, 12, 14
  contrasted to marble staircase, 13
  Finny's fall from, 23, 25, 31
  first jump, Gene and Finny's, 12
  symbolism, 14
trust, 7, 33, 58
truth, 29
Tunisian campaign, 47

W

war and blind anger, 50
War, the (World War II)
  arrival at Devon, 61
  Finny's changed theory about, 52, 53
  Finny's conspiracy theory about, 39–41,
    50, 61, 65
  Finny's early theory about, 15, 17
  Leper's opinions about, 50
water (symbolism), 31, 41, 45

Y

Yellow Peril, defined, 43

NOTES

_____
_____
_____
_____
_____
_____
_____
_____
_____
_____
_____
_____
_____
_____
_____
_____
_____
_____
_____
_____
_____
_____
_____
_____
_____

NOTES

NOTES

_____

_____

_____

_____

_____

_____

_____

_____

_____

_____

_____

_____

_____

_____

_____

_____

_____

_____

_____

_____

_____

_____

_____

NOTES

CliffsNotes

@ cliffsnotes.com

CliffsNotes

LITERATURE NOTES

Absalom, Absalom!
The Aeneid
Agamemnon
Alice in Wonderland
All the King's Men
All the Pretty Horses
All Quiet on the
    Western Front
All's Well &
    Merry Wives
American Poets of the
    20th Century
American Tragedy
Animal Farm
Anna Karenina
Anthem
Antony and Cleopatra
Aristotle's Ethics
As I Lay Dying
The Assistant
As You Like It
Atlas Shrugged
Autobiography of
    Ben Franklin
Autobiography of
    Malcolm X
The Awakening
Babbit
Bartleby & Benito
    Cereno
The Bean Trees
The Bear
The Bell Jar
Beloved
Beowulf
The Bible
Billy Budd & Typee
Black Boy
Black Like Me
Bleak House
Bless Me, Ultima
The Bluest Eye & Sula
Brave New World
The Brothers Karamazov

The Call of the Wild &
    White Fang
Candide
The Canterbury Tales
Catch-22
Catcher in the Rye
The Chosen
The Color Purple
Comedy of Errors…
Connecticut Yankee
The Contender
The Count of
    Monte Cristo
Crime and Punishment
The Crucible
Cry, the Beloved
    Country
Cyrano de Bergerac
Daisy Miller &
    Turn…Screw
David Copperfield
Death of a Salesman
The Deerslayer
Diary of Anne Frank
Divine Comedy-I.
    Inferno
Divine Comedy-II.
    Purgatorio
Divine Comedy-III.
    Paradiso
Doctor Faustus
Dr. Jekyll and Mr. Hyde
Don Juan
Don Quixote
Dracula
Electra & Medea
Emerson's Essays
Emily Dickinson Poems
Emma
Ethan Frome
The Faerie Queene
Fahrenheit 451
Far from the Madding
    Crowd
A Farewell to Arms
Farewell to Manzanar
Fathers and Sons
Faulkner's Short Stories

Faust Pt. I & Pt. II
The Federalist
Flowers for Algernon
For Whom the Bell Tolls
The Fountainhead
Frankenstein
The French
    Lieutenant's Woman
The Giver
Glass Menagerie &
    Streetcar
Go Down, Moses
The Good Earth
The Grapes of Wrath
Great Expectations
The Great Gatsby
Greek Classics
Gulliver's Travels
Hamlet
The Handmaid's Tale
Hard Times
Heart of Darkness &
    Secret Sharer
Hemingway's
    Short Stories
Henry IV Part 1
Henry IV Part 2
Henry V
House Made of Dawn
The House of the
    Seven Gables
Huckleberry Finn
I Know Why the
    Caged Bird Sings
Ibsen's Plays I
Ibsen's Plays II
The Idiot
Idylls of the King
The Iliad
Incidents in the Life of
    a Slave Girl
Inherit the Wind
Invisible Man
Ivanhoe
Jane Eyre
Joseph Andrews
The Joy Luck Club
Jude the Obscure

Julius Caesar
The Jungle
Kafka's Short Stories
Keats & Shelley
The Killer Angels
King Lear
The Kitchen God's Wife
The Last of the
    Mohicans
Le Morte d'Arthur
Leaves of Grass
Les Miserables
A Lesson Before Dying
Light in August
The Light in the Forest
Lord Jim
Lord of the Flies
The Lord of the Rings
Lost Horizon
Lysistrata & Other
    Comedies
Macbeth
Madame Bovary
Main Street
The Mayor of
    Casterbridge
Measure for Measure
The Merchant
    of Venice
Middlemarch
A Midsummer Night's
    Dream
The Mill on the Floss
Moby-Dick
Moll Flanders
Mrs. Dalloway
Much Ado About
    Nothing
My Ántonia
Mythology
Narr. …Frederick
    Douglass
Native Son
New Testament
Night
1984
Notes from the
    Underground

CliffsNotes
@ cliffsnotes.com

The Odyssey
Oedipus Trilogy
Of Human Bondage
Of Mice and Men
The Old Man and
 the Sea
Old Testament
Oliver Twist
The Once and
 Future King
One Day in the Life of
 Ivan Denisovich
One Flew Over the
 Cuckoo's Nest
100 Years of Solitude
O'Neill's Plays
Othello
Our Town
The Outsiders
The Ox Bow Incident
Paradise Lost
A Passage to India
The Pearl
The Pickwick Papers
The Picture of
 Dorian Gray
Pilgrim's Progress
The Plague
Plato's Euthyphro…
Plato's The Republic
Poe's Short Stories
A Portrait of the
 Artist…
The Portrait of a Lady
The Power and
 the Glory
Pride and Prejudice
The Prince
The Prince and
 the Pauper
A Raisin in the Sun
The Red Badge of
 Courage
The Red Pony
The Return of the
 Native
Richard II
Richard III

The Rise of
 Silas Lapham
Robinson Crusoe
Roman Classics
Romeo and Juliet
The Scarlet Letter
A Separate Peace
Shakespeare's
 Comedies
Shakespeare's Histories
Shakespeare's
 Minor Plays
Shakespeare's Sonnets
Shakespeare's Tragedies
Shaw's Pygmalion &
 Arms…
Silas Marner
Sir Gawain…Green
 Knight
Sister Carrie
Slaughterhouse-five
Snow Falling on Cedars
Song of Solomon
Sons and Lovers
The Sound and the Fury
Steppenwolf &
 Siddhartha
The Stranger
The Sun Also Rises
T.S. Eliot's Poems &
 Plays
A Tale of Two Cities
The Taming of the
 Shrew
Tartuffe, Misanthrope…
The Tempest
Tender Is the Night
Tess of the D'Urbervilles
Their Eyes Were
 Watching God
Things Fall Apart
The Three Musketeers
To Kill a Mockingbird
Tom Jones
Tom Sawyer
Treasure Island &
 Kidnapped
The Trial

Tristram Shandy
Troilus and Cressida
Twelfth Night
Ulysses
Uncle Tom's Cabin
The Unvanquished
Utopia
Vanity Fair
Vonnegut's Works
Waiting for Godot
Walden
Walden Two
War and Peace
Who's Afraid of
 Virginia…
Winesburg, Ohio
The Winter's Tale
The Woman Warrior
Worldly Philosophers
Wuthering Heights
A Yellow Raft in
 Blue Water

Setting Up a
 Windows 98
 Home Network
Shopping Online Safe
Upgrading and
 Repairing Your PC
Using Your First iMac
Using Your First PC
Writing Your First
 Computer Program

Check Out the All-New CliffsNotes Guides

TECHNOLOGY TOPICS

Balancing Your Check-
 book with Quicken
Buying and Selling
 on eBay
Buying Your First PC
Creating a Winning
 PowerPoint 2000
 Presentation
Creating Web Pages
 with HTML
Creating Your First
 Web Page
Exploring the World
 with Yahoo!
Getting on the Internet
Going Online with AOL
Making Windows 98
 Work for You

PERSONAL FINANCE TOPICS

Budgeting & Saving
 Your Money
Getting a Loan
Getting Out of Debt
Investing for the
 First Time
Investing in
 401(k) Plans
Investing in IRAs
Investing in
 Mutual Funds
Investing in the
 Stock Market
Managing Your Mone
Planning Your
 Retirement
Understanding
 Health Insurance
Understanding
 Life Insurance

CAREER TOPICS

Delivering a Winning
 Job Interview
Finding a Job
 on the Web
Getting a Job
Writing a Great Resum